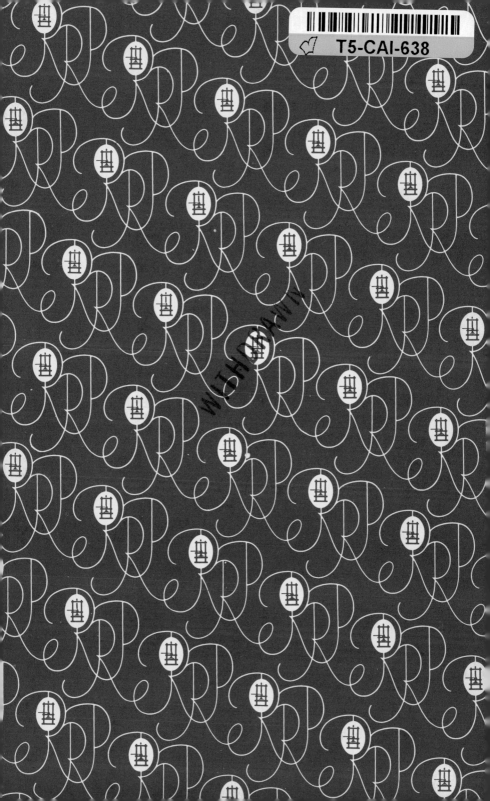

# YOUR FUTURE AS A RABBI

# YOUR FUTURE
## AS A
# RABBI

## A CALLING THAT COUNTS

RABBI ALFRED GOTTSCHALK, Ph.D.

RICHARDS ROSEN PRESS, INC., NEW YORK, N.Y. 10010

*Library of Congress Catalog Card Number:* 67-12679
*Dewey Decimal Classification:* 371.42

Published in 1967 by Richards Rosen Press, Inc.
29 East 21st Street, New York City, N.Y. 10010

*Copyright 1967 by Rabbi Alfred Gottschalk*

*First Edition*

*Manufactured in the United States of America*

## *About the Author*

Rabbi Alfred Gottschalk, Dean of the California School of the Hebrew Union College-Jewish Institute of Religion is also Professor of Bible and Jewish Religious Thought.

Dean Gottschalk was graduated from Brooklyn College (A.B.) with honors, and was ordained at the Hebrew Union College in Cincinnati (B.H.L., M.A.). He is also a graduate of the University of Southern California (Ph.D.). He has held scholarships and fellowships which have taken him to Europe and Israel. The latest of these was a State Department Study Grant for archaeological research in Israel, in 1963.

Interested and concerned with civic affairs locally and nationally, he serves on committees and boards such as the President's Committee on Equal Employment Opportunity, the Governor's Poverty Program Support Corps, Mayor Yorty's Community Advisory Committee of Los Angeles, Community Relations Committee of the Jewish Federation-Council, Committee on Religious Education of the Central Conference of American Rabbis, Religion and Labor Council of Los Angeles, American Jewish Committee, Los Angeles Association for Jewish Education, Los Angeles Jewish Historical Society, and the National Association of Temple Educators.

He is also a member of learned societies and educational groups. Among them are: The American Academy of Political and Social Science, American Academy of Religion, American Association for Higher Education, American Civil Liberties Union, Los Angeles World Affairs Council, Society for Biblical Literature and Exegesis, Israel Exploration Society, American Philosophical Society, American Association of University Pro-

5

fessors, and Delta Sigma Rho. He is the current President of the
Southern California Association of Liberal Rabbis.

Dr. Gottschalk has published widely and has taught at the
University of California at Los Angeles, Extension Division, and
has lectured at many of the universities on the West Coast.

With his wife Jeannie, and their children Marc Hillel and
Rachel Lisa, he presently resides in Westwood, California.

# Contents

# YOUR FUTURE AS A RABBI

## CHAPTER I

## Should I be a Rabbi?

### The Quality of Jewish Faith

Judaism as a religion and civilization represents one of the oldest and most vital philosophies of mankind. Mother faith to Christianity and Islam, it has nurtured a world-view which teaches the great truth that all men are brothers and that God is One. While these ideas are ancient they are still radical, for much of the world is still torn by distrust, inequality, and a strident inhumanity. Amid ancient and modern barbarities Judaism taught a doctrine of social justice and of the innate goodness of man. It championed man as created in God's image and not as some hapless lackey to the forces of nature, to deities of stone, or to human despots who demanded craven obedience. When these ideas of human dignity were first conceived in the heartland of civilization then known as Palestine, they shook the very foundations of society. Such thoughts were novel, and represented a new breakthrough in the development of the human conscience.

Because of Judaism's challenging and creative world outlook, it began to win spiritual adherents, and in time leaped the confines of the narrow geographic borders in which it was reared to become a world religion of immense force. Christianity and Islam, which based themselves on biblical teachings, brought the insights of Judaism to the most benighted and obscure hamlets of the world. Great centers of civilization also learned of Judaism for, in addition to the offshoots of the Jewish faith, Judaism itself remained vibrant and creative. From the destruction of the Second Temple, by the Roman legions in the year 70 of this era, to the rebirth of the Jewish State in 1947, Jews settled in a vast diaspora. No hub of intellectual, mercantile, or cultural activity was devoid of their presence. Wherever life was pulsating, there Jews brought their traditions and historic faith. Judaism, because it was a universal religion, was portable, and so Jews infused their environment with the religious truths that had first been revealed to them on Sinai and on the other great heights and deserts of the Holy Land. There, prophets saw visions of a world in which men need not "learn war anymore," humane priests taught the commandments of Moses, and sages probed the meaning of human existence.

Judaism remained an exciting faith because it successfully fought off the temptation to become preoccupied with other-worldliness. Certainly, the problems of an after-life, immortality, heaven, and hell were studied, and ideas about these issues hotly debated. Basically, however, Judaism focused on the issues of the living. Its feet remained firmly planted on the ground. Judaism never lost its nerve or despaired of solving the problems of man in this world. That is why it retained its relevance even in the most tumultuous revolutions and intellectual upheavals.

That is also why contemporary America is so vitally interested in Jewish life and thought, and so many books and plays on Jewish subjects are being written and widely read. The great interest in the Jew and in Judaism in America presents an interesting puzzle. It is obvious from the many sociological studies that are being conducted that there is a shrinking difference in attitudes between the American Jew and his non-Jewish counterpart. And yet, precisely at this moment the American public is studying the Jews most intently. The reason may very well be that put forth in a *Time* magazine editorial recently: "In an age of 'alienation' the Jew is looked to as an expert in estrangement —the perpetual outsider who knows how to keep warm out there." But that is not all. The new spate of books depicting Jewish life also portrays a Jewish world-view which is compelling. There is a tenacity in Judaism to bring light and truth to the world, often against incredible odds.

In the cruel pangs of their recent suffering, Jews have maintained with Anne Frank-like simplicity that, despite all, man still has great capacity for goodness within him. How wistful such a hope must have seemed amid the Nazi atrocities. And yet hundreds of thousands of Jews went to their death with words of hope and prayer on their lips. "I believe with perfect faith," they chanted the old Maimonidean principle, ". . . that the Messiah will yet come. Though he may tarry, still, I await him." How absurd these Jews must have seemed to their murderers and perhaps even to themselves. They hoped beyond the limits of hope in man's redemption from evil. But that is what a Jew does. He declares to be God's fool even in a world where Satan seems to hold sway. There is something schooled into the Jew by his faith which will not rest while the forces of destruction are loose in the world. Judaism instills a compulsion to work for the long-envisioned society, "Where each shall sit under his vine and under his fig tree and none shall make him afraid." Perhaps it is this quality in the faith of Judaism which so captivates modern America, once again restless about its own dreams and ideals.

## THE RELEVANCY OF THE RABBINIC CALLING

While the Jewish faith requires all of Israel to strive toward its espoused goals, there have always been those who by virtue of leadership qualities emerged to shape Judaism's destiny. Those who view Judaism predominantly as a religion have looked to a certain kind of leadership for guidance. For over two thousand years the Jewish people has relied upon its rabbis to be teachers *par excellence* of the Jewish tradition. The term *rabbi* means "my teacher" or "my master" and was used to designate one who was an accomplished scholar of Torah, both in its written and oral tradition, and who was ordained. His accreditation was attested to by his ordination (*semikhah*), granted by an older scholar of unquestioned learning.*

* Such was the procedure in Palestine in the period of the *Tannaim* (70-217 C.E.), the teachers of the Mishnah. In Babylonia those who taught the Mishnah, the authoritative law code compiled by Rabbi Judah, the Prince (135-217 C.E.), were called *Amoraim,* expounders of the Mishnah. A teacher of the law ordained in that community was called *rav,* which also means "master" and "teacher." The title of an ordained Jewish scholar today follows the Palestinian designation.

Since the formative period, in which the rabbinate evolved, there have been several major phases of its development. The rabbinate of today is permeated by the ideals of its historic proto- types, but new in style and character. It must be made clear that the rabbinate is not a priesthood. While there are rabbis who are Priests (*Kohanim*), there are many who are not. By and large, rabbis are Jewish laymen (*Yisroel*). The rites and ceremonies they perform are, from the Jewish legal aspect, permissible to any knowledgeable Israelite. Marriage ceremonies, funerals, baby namings, leading public worship are the prerogatives of any learned Jew. The leader of public worship or ceremonial was the representative of the community before God. Rarely in tradi- tion, except on stated occasions, did the rabbi of the community assume the role of precentor. Regrettably, the temper of modern times has greatly reduced the number of Jews who are sufficiently aware of the legal and ceremonial practices to perform these sacred rites themselves. Today, the rabbi's role is virtually that of religious official who performs all the functions previously ac- corded as a privilege to any worthy Jew. In a later chapter we shall see how this development came about, but suffice it to say that even in his new capacity the rabbi is not accorded the office of priest.

The rabbi is not an intermediary between God and man. No Jew prays through his rabbi. The rabbi has no right to pardon sins or hear confession. The rabbi's views are his opinions, his considered judgements, or even verdicts based on his understand- ing of Jewish law; they are not indisputable dogma or a vehicle to heaven. While there are significant differences among Ortho- dox (very traditional), Conservative, and Reform rabbis as to the understanding of their calling, none would claim for himself absolute authority in the interpretation of Torah. In American Jewish life the various enclaves of rabbis have developed plat- forms, guidelines, and norms of religious life, but these organiza- tions have always been cognizant that the American Jew lives in a voluntaristic society. The American Jew may put himself under traditional discipline or orthodox Jewish law, but no one can compel him to do so. In this environment of freedom, a premium has been put on the rabbi's ability to convince the modern Jew through sermons, lectures, and discussions. Religiosity cannot be coerced or commanded. It can only be induced through conviction maturing into firm belief.

The emancipation of the modern pulpit which made the rabbinic calling into a potent force was the end product of a hard and courageous struggle. The modern rabbi maintained that Judaism had something to say about the rights of labor, about war and peace, about the growing alienation of man in a technological society. Judaism had some well-tested philosophies to apply to the mounting revolution in morals, to the problems of education and human relations. Questions were raised by an increasing number of Jewish college students on the compatibility of Judaism with science and to the insights of the new psychology discovered by Sigmund Freud. Rabbis followed the advice of the ingenious Ben Bag Bag of the Mishnah who advised, "Turn it (the Torah) and turn it over again, for everything is in it . . ." Tradition and interpretation once again had to be expanded so that the new generation of Jews would not be "included out." The message of Judaism had once more to be brought into the marketplace of ideas and faiths which ventured forth to wrestle with the problems and perils of the modern world.

A generation of American rabbis dared to break the conventional role of the rabbi as resource scholar expounding law and lore to a dwindling remnant of Talmud-trained Jews. The Hillel and the Jewish Chautauqua programs brought rabbis to the campuses. Jews and Christians began to confront one another as equals trying to understand each other's faith. Discussions which began at times with condescending tolerance developed into real dialogues, reversing two thousand years of intermittent animosity. The rabbi was in the forefront of these developments, often initiating bold new programs and approaches.

There were giants in the American rabbinate, for it was an age of intellectual and moral frontiersmanship. Men hewed out

paths for Judaism where none existed before. Of one of the
greatest of American rabbis of the past generation, Stephen S.
Wise, the learned Rabbi Solomon Goldman said, "Wises were
born to rule Empires; all that Jewry could offer was a pulpit."
Wise made much of his pulpit. He propelled it into the chancel-
leries of the world. Through him and others like him, Judaism
with its dynamism, sense of justice, and restlessness with the
"as is," once more spoke to the world. The modern rabbi, to
paraphrase Ezekiel, sought that which was lost, brought back
that which was driven away, bound up that which was broken,
and strengthened that which was sick. The great legacy of the
ancient rabbinate was given new coinage by bold and courageous
men who sought to mold the modern Jew and his world to the
eternal ideals of Judaism.

It is the essence of tradition that worth-while values and institutions be transmitted. That is why each year several hundred
seminarians, newly ordained, enter the Jewish world to renew
the traditions of the rabbinate and to leave their own impress
upon it. As a teacher of rabbis I have seen some outstanding
young men who, in time, will rise to the challenges of this era
and bring the message of Judaism anew to this generation of
Jews. Seminaries cannot mass-produce Stephen Wises or Abba
Hillel Silvers. They grow to maturity in novel circumstances and,
in time, the new giants will rear their lionized heads and we will
know that other great teachers of Judaism are on the horizon.

The intellectual and spiritual commitments required of the
rabbi limit the available candidates for this calling. Yet it is my
feeling that there are many young men of idealism and worth
who will ask themselves the question, "Should I be a rabbi?" The
cut of man who can rise to the great challenges of the rabbinate
is not ordinary, and that is another reason why the fraternity
of rabbis, be it Reform, Conservative, or Orthodox, is not large.

But what of those rabbinic candidates who enter the seminaries? What is their background and what motivates them?
Many of the applicants to rabbinical seminaries decide to become

rabbis because they have been inspired in their youth or on the college campus by some outstanding rabbinic personality. They seek to emulate someone whom they trust and for whom they have respect. Such candidates consider themselves disciples of a great teacher. There are other candidates whose initial impetus to enter the field came from other considerations. Orthodox young men, who were reared in *yeshivot* (all-day parochial schools) and whose total environment is Jewish, may have considered the rabbinate as the most logical extension of their training and intellectual and religious pursuits. The rabbinate appears to this segment of candidates as the most natural environment for the enlargement of their Jewish learning, and for the opportunity to serve the largest segment of Jewish life which claims to be traditional or orthodox.

Still others enter the rabbinic academies because of personal experiences in religious camping. There are many encampments, sponsored by all religious groups, whose programs focus upon providing an intensive and wholesome environment in which Judaism is lived naturally and daily. This encounter has a transforming effect on a young person: life values often fall into place and Judaism's message to the world becomes a passionate concern. From this experience also, the rabbinate may seem as a clear choice which will make it possible to devote oneself to a lifetime of service.

There is yet another clear category of rabbinical student who is more frequently found in the Reform and Conservative seminaries. This is a core of hard-thinking young people, who may or may not have come from a religious environment; or having come from one, have broken discipline with it to seek their own way in the world. They may be fervent Zionists or non-Zionists, mystical or rational by temperament. The *meaning* of Judaism marks their quest. They look to their ancestral faith as one which needs to address itself to the burning issues of our time; it must have the bite of relevance. In their view, tradition cannot be produced to attest to its own validity. Existence and reason, as well as tradition, represent the criteria for the evaluation of Jewish belief, custom, and ceremony. Often, such candidates know little or no Hebrew and have but the faintest grasp of Jewish history. Yet they have a hunger for knowledge and constitute a great challenge to the seminaries. It is not uncommon for such highly motivated students to reach the very top of their class by the time of ordination.

Amid the great diversity of backgrounds that the candidates bring with them, there are some vital and irreducible common denominators. While a student's God-concept may not yet be fixed, he acknowledges by his thoughts and deeds the presence of divine power in his life. God is a reality to him about which he thinks as well as to whom he prays. Performance of *mitzvot* (acts originating from religious commitment) represent his true inner being. These may range from putting on *tefilin* (phylacteries) to participating in a civil rights or peace march. Theological problems of all sorts should interest him. A theological student in a Jewish seminary must master a vast intellectual tradition in which difference of viewpoint is abundantly evident. He must be prepared to stretch his mind to understand the issues involved, and evidence a passion for the pursuit of truth. Looming as perhaps the most immediately relevant common denominator is the student's involvement with the destiny of his people. The Jewish people are the tangible expression of the success or failure of Judaism. The survival of Judaism through Jews must genuinely engage his every waking moment. And in his sleep he must dare to dream his people's timeless vision of a just and peaceful world, in which the program of Judaism has been expanded to world-wide dimensions.

There is room in the rabbinic fraternity for young men for whom these concerns are vital and who would make them the occupation of their daily life. The rabbinate can be one of the most useful, creative, and satisfying careers. There is no end of good work and programming that can be done. There is no dearth of pulpits or of educational or institutional opportunities requiring spiritual leadership.

CAREER OPPORTUNITIES

The modern rabbinate is composed of men who have been ordained in Orthodox, Conservative, or Reform seminaries. There are rabbis in America who are graduates of great European *yeshivot* and seminaries. There are also men who hold private ordination. Those in the last category are usually Orthodox rabbis. To became eligible for ordination as a rabbi, a candidate must complete a course of study which varies in length depending upon his previous knowledge and the requirements of the seminary of his choice. Each of the branches of Judaism makes certain theological emphases, and one may properly expect these to be reflected in the curricula of the seminaries they sponsor.

There are great similarities of vocational opportunity which hold true for any ordained rabbi, irrespective of the seminary from which he graduated. The largest number of rabbis actively engaged in full-time rabbinic work is found in congregational situations. Because of the growing number of Jewish families affiliated with congregations, senior rabbis engage recent graduates to be their assistants. A good assistantship affords the younger colleague great opportunity to learn the intricacies of his profession from his seasoned senior. Many assistants supervise the religious school and share pastoral and sermonic duties. There are assistant positions that may grow into associate posts if the opportunity is present and the colleagues find themselves compatible.

Increasingly, there are other opportunities available for rabbis in religiously oriented institutions. Each of the major branches of Judaism has national congregational organizations. In the Reform movement, for example, the Union of American Hebrew Congregations engages rabbis as regional directors for its various councils. In addition, rabbis direct national education, youth, camping, religious action, interfaith, and synagogal activities. The Orthodox and Conservative movements afford similar opportunities for such administrative positions. Hillel Foundations engage great numbers of rabbis to direct the programs of Jewish college youth on university campuses throughout the United States and Canada. In some instances, a Hillel directorship carries with it the opportunity to do teaching in Judaica on the campus to which the rabbi is assigned. There are growing numbers of seminary and university teaching opportunities developing. Full-time chairs in Jewish Studies and in Hebrew language and literature are being established at a rate which continues to dramatize the lack of qualified candidates to occupy these positions. To fill these vacancies, university administrators are regularly turning to scholarly rabbis.

Because the training of the rabbi makes him an expert in Jewish lore, many Jewish communal organizations engage rabbis as their executive directors. Bureaus of Jewish Education, the B'nai B'rith, the American Jewish Committee, the American Jewish Congress, the National Jewish Welfare Board, the National Conference of Christians and Jews, all have at some time or another employed rabbi-administrators. The various Zionist organizations and youth and camping institutes constantly seek rabbis in a professional capacity to carry out their programs. The military chaplaincy has become the life's work of a number of rabbis, as has the institutional chaplaincy. In the latter instance, rabbis are engaged, usually through the Jewish Federations of their community or through the National Jewish Welfare Board, to serve as spiritual leaders and counselors to patients in hospitals of all kinds, in orphanages, prisons, and homes for the aged. There are now also a striking number of rabbinic opportunities abroad. Congregations in New Zealand, Australia, South Africa, South America, Great Britain, and Israel are avidly seeking candidates to fill their pulpits and administrative positions in Jewish communal agencies.

By far the greatest number of pulpit vacancies exists in the United States itself. Several hundred congregations lack professional religious leadership. Because available candidates for pulpits cluster in and about great metropolitan centers with large Jewish populations, smaller communities often go unserved. If they are fortunate in securing the services of a theological student in training, their need is somewhat lessened. The number of students now graduating from the major seminaries is clearly inadequate to meet the growing needs of the synagogues, temples, and service agencies. At no period in Jewish history has the time been more opportune to increase the "disciples of the wise" so that Judaism might be more nobly served.

## The Status of the Profession

In 1954 the American Jewish community concluded its tercentenary celebration. The occasion elicited many studies of American Jewry. Among numerous projects undertaken was a study by the Jewish Statistical Bureau under the direction of H. S. Linfield on "The Rabbis of the United States." The study examined (1) the number of rabbis in the United States— Orthodox, Conservative, and Reform; (2) rabbinical training; (3) secular education; (4) areas of service.

The study indicated that in the first two centuries of Jewish history in the United States, beginning with 1654, the growth in the number of rabbis was relatively moderate. This situation changed drastically during the second half of the nineteenth century so that by 1900, 526 rabbis were counted in the *Jewish Directory*. In 1954, the *Registry of American Rabbis* contained the roster of 4,257 names. This represented the largest number of rabbis ever recorded in the United States. A total of 651 rabbis were affiliated with the association of Reform Rabbis, known as the Central Conference of American Rabbis; 529 rabbis, with the association of Conservative rabbis, the Rabbinical Assembly of America; and 1,305 rabbis, with three associations of Orthodox rabbis: the Union of Orthodox Rabbis of the United States and Canada, the Rabbinical Council of America, and the Rabbinical Alliance of America. This grouping indicates that 2,485 rabbis were affiliated with the major national associations of rabbis.

Historically speaking, the Central Conference of American Rabbis is the oldest of the rabbinic associations, created in 1899 by Isaac Mayer Wise. The Rabbinical Assembly of America was formed in 1901; the Union of Orthodox Rabbis of the United States and Canada, in 1902; the Rabbinical Council of America, 1923; the Rabbinical Alliance of America, 1944. The standards of these associations admit to membership only such men as are ordained by recognized seminaries and authorities, and who comport themselves with the highest standards of the profession.

There are additional associations of rabbis which are smaller in number and influence which do not have uniform professional standards for admission. Some 1,470 rabbis involved in congregational or allied fields were not members of the major national associations. Of the 1,470 unaffiliated rabbis, a total of 792 were trained and ordained abroad. Another group of unaffiliated men consisted of some 302 former rabbis who were engaged in other occupations.

In percentage figures, 15.3 per cent of the affiliated rabbis were members of the Reform movement; 12.4 per cent, of the Conservative movement; and 30.7 per cent, of the three associations of Orthodox rabbis; 15.9 per cent constituted the sizeable body of unaffiliated rabbis who were trained and ordained in the United States; 18.6 per cent, trained and ordained abroad; and 7.1 per cent were engaged in secular occupations.

Making allowances for reasonable growth in the national rabbinic organizations, one may estimate that today there are 5,000 rabbis in the United States, of which the Orthodox are still most numerous, while the Conservative and Reform have remained relatively equal in number.

The salaries of rabbis are dependent upon many factors. The 1954 survey showed that a total of 2,517 rabbis were affiliated with Jewish congregations in which the rabbi was "the principle functionary, ministering to the religious needs of the congregation and the community." For this largest category of men in the active rabbinate, salaries are often dependent on the size and affluence of the congregation. Beginning salaries in 1966 ranged in the vicinity of $8,000 to $8,500. Of course, there are rabbis who began at lower salaries and others who commenced their careers at higher remuneration. Average salaries in smaller congregations or communities range from $8,000 to $10,000 for rabbis who have some rabbinic experience. The usual salary of a rabbi in the field for a period of ten years may range from $12,000 to $18,000; and in large congregations, $25,000 a year and higher. However, opportunities of the latter category are limited and are usually won by the most prominent men in the profession. On the other hand, there are many important rabbis who elect to remain in smaller congregations and at smaller salary scales because they are convinced that they can render a more valuable service in such an environment. Rabbis may also augment their income by emoluments, from officiating at ceremonies and at rituals such as weddings and funerals. However, many rabbis donate such emoluments to the temple or to a charitable fund within the temple which is distributed at the rabbi's discretion.

Salary schedules for rabbis who specialize in Jewish community service are difficult to obtain, since they vary so much with the particular agency. More often than not, where responsibilities are comparable, salaries are competitive with those paid by congregations. The 1954 survey indicated that 22.2 per cent, or 944 rabbis, were engaged in full-time specialized Jewish community service. Included in this category are the chaplaincy, both military and nonmilitary, the field of Jewish education, and Jewish social and welfare work.

As in every profession, there are those who for a period of time are unemployed. The reasons may vary from the problems of professional competence to temporary illness. One hundred and forty-eight rabbis, or 3.5 per cent of the profession, were unemployed. It was also noted that 166 rabbis, or 3.9 per cent, were retired.

These statistical tables would indicate reasonable stability in the field with a majority of active rabbis in congregational situations.

PAST AND PRESENT—THE CHANGING ROLE OF THE RABBI

It is still true, other opportunities notwithstanding, that most rabbinic students hope to become congregational rabbis. Whether the candidates be Orthodox, Conservative or Reform, the pulpit represents the historical medium for imparting the teachings of Judaism. There has been, of late, considerable discussion on the changing role of the rabbi. Books have been written on the failure of the American rabbi and on his growing loss of status within the organized Jewish community. Articles and essays have appeared in popular and learned journals attempting to define precisely what it is that the congregational rabbi on the scene today is expected to do in order to perform both his historic function as a teacher of Judaism and as a minister to an ever-growing following of synagogue-affiliated Jews. Much of this discussion reflects the growing pains of an ancient calling trying to adjust itself to the climate of modern life and to the new contours of burgeoning communities. Recently Rabbi Norman Hirsh of Seattle, Washington, preached a sermon to his congregation entitled, "What is a Rabbi?" In his sermon, he made the following observations:

I can think of 14 important task I perform:

Visiting the sick
Counseling the troubled
Conducting services
Preaching
Supervising the religious school
Teaching children—both Confirmation Class and Bar Mitzvah
    students
Adult education
Officiating at weddings, funerals, etc.
Interfaith speaking in the community
Social action in the community
Temple administration
Building a temple or worrying about new facilities

Temple programming—including the bulletin
Teaching converts

The number of tasks the rabbi performs is staggering. Unless he is wise and resolute, able to say no as well as yes, he will be totally fragmented.

I am not essentially an administrator, a builder of temples, a counselor, an ambassador to the non-Jews, or any of the dozen other functions I perform. I am a rabbi, a Jew trained in scholarship, and my central task is to learn and to teach.

It is unquestionably the temper of modern times that has created the condition in which rabbis and congregants ask themselves the question which is also the title of Rabbi Hirsh's sermon, "What *is* a Rabbi?"

In order for us to carry the discussion further, it would indeed be helpful to look at some historic notes on the origin and development of the rabbinate. As has previously been indicated, the history of rabbinic ordination goes back to the first centuries of our era. Particularly after the destruction of the Second Temple in the year 70 was it necessary to determine upon whom the mantle of leadership should lie. It fell upon a remarkable group of rabbis deeply learned in the law, whose credential was their *semikhah,* or ordination. These rabbis played such a vital part in the perpetuation and enlargement of Judaism that in the second century of the common era, when the Emperor Hadrian sought to destroy this ancient faith, he prohibited the ordination of rabbis. The penalty for the ordainer and the ordained, if discovered, was death. The city in which the ordination took place was to be put to the sword.

Jewish history records that many of the great rabbis, as well as their students, jeopardized their lives to maintain the practice of ordination because it had come to mean the lawful transfer of authority from one generation of scholars to the next. For example, the aged Judah ben Baba gathered five disciples to a secluded spot between the cities of Usha and Shefaram to ordain them. The group was betrayed by informers and Roman soldiers soon closed in. Before the legionnaires arrived, ben Baba ordained the disciples who barely escaped their tormentors. Their great teacher, however, was caught and, according to the Talmud, Roman soldiers drove three hundred javelins into his body. Judah, fully aware that discovery meant certain death, elected nevertheless to sacrifice his life for Torah so that Torah might endure.

Prior to the creation of the rabbinate as an institution, there were three leadership types clearly delineated in the Bible. The book of Jeremiah states, "For instruction shall not perish from the priest, nor counsel from the wise, nor the word from the prophet." In the rabbinate these three functions of Jewish leadership were integrated and thereby also perpetuated. It was Thomas Carlyle who proclaimed in his *Heroes and Hero Worship* that "universal history, the history of what man has accomplished in this world, is at the bottom the history of the great men who have worked here." This is certainly true of the architects of Judaism—the priests, prophets and sages—who prepared the mind-set of the Jewish people so that it might become a bearer of truth to the world.

The prophet was a dynamic leader, who represented no societal institution nor vested interest—but truth as his mind and heart understood it. The prophets believed that their message emanated from divine inspiration and from a confrontation with God. The Hebrew prophet addressed himself to the question of what it was that God desired of man and of human society. One of them answered in the sublime language, "Only to do justice, to love mercy, and to walk humbly with thy God." The Hebrew prophets emerge as God-intoxicated men who gave leadership to their people by their understanding of religious obligation, manifest in the conduct of their lives. This sort of dynamic leader sprang from no particular caste. Aristocracy of birth was not a prerequisite for his mission. He enjoyed no special privileges in society for his role. To the contrary, often he suffered penalties for the uncompromising way in which he spoke the truth.

The priesthood was another category of leadership, perhaps best designated as "symbolic leadership." Priests fulfilled their duties often as official representatives at the local or national shrines. "Torah" represents the priests' concern. The priest was an expert in ritual matters who knew the distinction between the holy and the profane. The priest showed concern for order, legalism, and religious conduct. Ahad Ha-Am, in an essay entitled "Priest and Prophet," brilliantly points out the additional function of the priesthood in early Hebrew culture. Charged with the task of translating prophetic ideals into the fabric of society, the priest often acted as mediator betwen the status quo and the new idea whose time had come.

The sage was yet another type of teacher—the wise man at whose hands counsel was sought. Unlike the prophet and the priest, the sage approached the problems of the world in pragmatic terms. He sought to perceive the dynamic in human relationships and then project modes of conduct in harmony with the law of God and the law of the universe.

The rabbis synthesized these three qualities of leadership and created a powerful composite, able to respond to the needs of their time. The rabbis were a scholar-class who belonged to a movement within Judaism known as the Pharisees. In Rabbi Leo Baeck's estimation, the Pharisees comprised "the people's party." The rabbis waged a relentless battle for the status of the individual Jew. To this Jew, the rabbis offered a deed-oriented religion which also imposed learning upon him as an obligation of his Jewish heritage. This approach enabled the Pharisees to create a revolutionary religious, social, and educational institution called the synagogue, whose threefold purpose as a house of assembly, a house of prayer, and a house of study survives to this day.

A Pharisaic sage was called a *Talmid Hakham*. It was to him that the Jew looked with confidence for interpretations relating to educational, spiritual, and legal matters. The *Talmid Hakham* was an authority figure, not only because he was learned in Judaic matters but because he was a rounded scholar, a man of the world, able to concern himself with secular as well as religious matters. In the period of the Tannaim (70-217 C.E.) ordained *Talmide Hakhamim* were not compensated because of their title as rabbi. All the talmudic sages earned their livelihood through some other occupation. The rabbis of this period were conscious of the teaching, "Make not of the Torah a crown wherewith to aggrandize yourself, not a spade with which to dig." The sage Hillel was a woodchopper; Shammai, a builder; Joshua ben Hananiah, a blacksmith; Akiba, a shepherd; Johanan, a cobbler. Still others were tailors, water carriers, linguists, poets, astronomers, or students of natural history. Some were physicians, and others farmers and merchants. During the talmudic period the chief interest of the rabbis was the *halakhah* (law). Their *semikhah* was a judicial degree which conferred special status upon the rabbi who concerned himself with the teaching and adjudication of the law. There were also men whose ordination designated that they were preachers and teachers of the *agadah,* the nonlegal portions of the Talmud. The sermon was a regular part of the Sabbath morning service in the talmudic period, where *agadah* was used for the purpose of public instruction.

By the middle of the fourteenth century, the tradition of not receiving compensation for rabbinic services underwent a radical change. After the terrible plague of the Black Death, the scholars who survived the catastrophe, and who lacked capital, found themselves compelled to make the teaching of the Torah the means of their livelihood. Beginning with the fifteenth century, the rabbinate gradually became a profession. With rabbinic irony, and cognizant of the ancient teaching that one should not be compensated for teaching Torah, the rabbi's salary was defined as *sekhar battalah,* compensation for being prevented from engaging in a gainful occupation. Rabbinic emoluments, however, were minimal and many rabbis maintained themselves through additional occupations, stipends from communal taxes, and fees received for sitting as judges. It was also the rabbi's responsibility to maintain an academy, to teach in it, and to examine the students.

The rabbi was required to personally set an example of devotion to study. It was not unusual for him to spend most of his waking hours poring over the intricate legal codes and other rabbinic literature, so that he might be able to answer, on the basis of precedents established within that literature, questions of law posed to him. If he was quite expert, other communities would consult him in writing by sending questions of law, to which he would respond. This body of legal material, known as the Responsa Literature, contains case law which he had to know in order to fulfill his function as judge and arbiter. The rabbi also became the molder of communal institutions and the guardian of moral conduct. It was his obligation to motivate people to acts of charity and to support the welfare institutions created. The rabbi would preach on special occasions and was accorded the honor of reading services on certain holidays. These enormous responsibilities of the rabbi could only be met through devotion and, at times, through great personal sacrifice.

Often romanticized, but hardly ever by those who were compelled to live in it, the ghetto presented another distinct chapter in the development of the rabbinate. Originally the ghetto came into being in the late Middle Ages when Jews, through legal enactments, were segregated in certain areas of cities and towns. The ghetto was established in Germany after the Black Death in 1348-1349 and in Venice in 1516. It created an isolationist type of Judaism which, nevertheless, enabled the Jew to survive this critical period of his history. While Judaism was never monolithic in ideology, there always was a vast central core of law and tradition to which Jews subscribed. In the ghetto, conformity to that tradition was mandatory. Within the ghetto there was self-government, which commanded the allegiance of those who dwelt within the confines of its walls. While the ghetto created inner cohesiveness and loyalty to the Jewish group, it remained intellectually sealed off from the rest of the world. There emerged in the ghetto the *Rav* who usually was as impressive in his appearance as he was in his learning. It was his task to act as judge in lawsuits and to answer questions of ritual. On two occasions during the year he delivered sermons. The *Rav* became the symbol of Jewish piety and learning and was greatly revered for these qualities. In Eastern Europe, until the dawn of the twentieth century and in some communities to this very day, the *Rav* represents the embodiment of authority in matters pertaining to the Jewish tradition.

Moses Mendelssohn (1729-1786), the father of the Jewish Enlightenment in Germany, sought to bring an end to ghetto-type isolation. Mendelssohn said that Judaism could only survive in the modern world if it became a religious persuasion whose truths were rational and universal. In his book, *Jerusalem* (1783), Mendelssohn developed an approach for the separation of church and state. The state, he reasoned, may not legislate what a man must believe; it cannot regulate the ideas or the convictions of its citizens. Conversely, religion must be sheared of all political power; its force must be moral, influencing the state by instruction and persuasion. It was Mendelssohn's theory to separate the powers of church and state so that religion could flourish freely without external coercion.

Until the time of the French Revolution the conditions outside the ghetto held no temptations for intellectual or social exploration. This state of affairs changed drastically when Napoleon Bonaparte demolished the ghettos on his march to conquest. The French Revolution and the ideals it held out of "liberty, equality and fraternity" created a most attractive world of which to be a part. At least this is what was thought by the most gifted and ambitious members of the community now daring to reach out into the larger world. In 1807, attempting to consolidate the gains of the revolution, Napoleon convened a high court, which was called the Sanhedrin. He patterned it after the Palestinian Sanhedrin of antiquity, so that its authority would be unquestioned in the eyes of the newly emancipated Jews. His purpose in calling the Jewish notables together was to get the sanction of the organized Jewish community for his plan of shearing all religion of the power it previously had to adjudicate civil law. Napoleon wanted religion removed from politics, and the Sanhedrin he called agreed to his terms on behalf of the Jewish communities under his rule.

The rabbis who had judged matters which were now to be tried by the civil courts lost considerable authority over their co-religionists. No longer could Jewish affairs be decided solely according to *halakhah,* particularly in the domain of personal status, e.g., laws of marriage, divorce, and inheritance. While previously it was impossible for a Jew to be married outside the authority of *halakhah,* he now could avail himself of a civil magistrate if he so desired. The state, in effect, protected the newly emancipated Jew from *halakhah* so that he could, if he chose, sever himself completely from his religious community.

Mendelssohn's theory and Bonaparte's politics conspired to denude Judaism of all of its national qualities and beliefs, and made it into a religion, a persuasion. This was the price of emancipation and of citizenship. The formula that was worked out in Germany and France became also the formula for religious life in America. In fact, it is only in America that some significant form of separation of church and state truly exists. Nowhere in the world does religious pluralism flourish as here, and nowhere in the world is Mendelssohn's plea for the separation of church and state more significant.

The far-reaching philosophical premises advocated by Mendelssohn and the practical enforcement of these ideas for other reasons by Bonaparte could not fail but throw the traditional rabbinate into a turmoil. The question of what the rabbinate was to become arose at this juncture in history and it is a question that is still being posed today. The Orthodox rabbinate, which has never made peace with the separation of powers, has held on to every conceivable thread of *halakhic* authority. For the Orthodox, all *halakhah* is divinely revealed law. To surrender *halakhah* even in civil matters is grudgingly done. For example, no divorced Orthodox person may remarry another Orthodox person unless a religious, as well as a civil, divorce has been secured. The argument runs that since marriage is a sacrament sealed by *halakhah,* it cannot be abrogated except through *halakhah.* The Conservative rabbinate has of late developed a similar position on the principles involved in such a question. The Reform rabbinate broke, in principle, with the binding authority of *halakhah;* it looks to civil authority to adjudicate questions arising out of the laws of personal status.

It was inevitable that in Europe, under these pressures, a new kind of rabbinate was to emerge. Rabbinic schools had to be created to train rabbis who could preserve Judaism in the modern world. In 1829, in Padua, a rabbinic college was opened where, by royal decree, candidates for the rabbinate needed a doctorate in philosophy. It was in Germany, however, upon the urging of the great Reform Rabbi Abraham Geiger, that a plan was developed for the creation of a Jewish theological faculty to be affiliated with a German university. Geiger felt that a seminary should be located in the heart of the intellectual life of the times, and not be isolated and exclusive. Geiger's plan for a liberal seminary did not immediately pan out. The first seminary was established in Breslau, in 1854, and was representative of what we call Conservative Judaism. Its director was the great scholar, Zacharias Frankel, who opposed radical reform as well as ultra-Orthodoxy. The curriculum of the seminary was comprehensive and the subjects were taught with scientific thoroughness.

In 1869, Geiger and Ludwig Philippson once again pleaded for the creation of a Jewish theological faculty, where men of different religious viewpoints would occupy the important chairs of the institution. It was proposed that there should be full freedom in academic research and in the presentation of Jewish thought. It was also argued that no conformity of religious practice was to be required of the students. The major emphasis was on Jewish knowledge and its scientific pursuit. The seminary opened in 1872 and shaped the thought of Reform Judaism. It was called the *Hochschule* and later it was known as the

*Lehranstalt fuer die Wissenschaft des Judentums* (Academy for the Science of Judaism).

In 1873, Dr. Israel Hildesheimer of Berlin established the Orthodox rabbinical seminary which became a prototype of the Isaac Elhanan Yeshivah of New York, as Breslau had been for the Jewish Theological Seminary of America, and the *Lehranstalt* for the Hebrew Union College. It was on American soil, particularly after the decimation of the European Jewish communities in World War II, that the ideologies of modern Judaism came to maturity.

It is evident that the nucleus of the role of the modern rabbi was present throughout the various phases of the development of the rabbinate as an institution. In the modern world, to all of the various traditional functions of the rabbi, there had to be added the function of relating Jewish life and Jewish institutions to the rigors of the scientific age and its outlook.

The present-day emphases of the rabbinate in America grew out of the principle of voluntarism in religious association. On these shores, a unique type of Jewish communal life developed. Autonomous Jewish congregations emerged in all branches of Judaism. Each congregation reserved for itself the right and the privilege of electing its own rabbi. From the ultra-Orthodox to the most Reform, this freedom is still cherished today. There are presently voluntary congregational organizations, such as the United Synagogue, the Union of American Hebrew Congregations, the Union of Orthodox Jewish Congregations of America, as well as national placement commissions for each of these congregational units. Normally, rabbis select congregations whose pattern of religious practice is closest to their own viewpoint. It is not uncommon, however, to find that a rabbi whose ideology was initially mismatched with that of his congregation is able, over the years, to weld his viewpoint and that of the congregation closer together.

The modern congregation which emerged in America demanded a religious program which would update Judaism and enable the Jew to live as a Jew in his emancipated status. As in past history, it inevitably fell to the rabbi to develop within such an environment a viable Jewish life. Modern congregations tend to be self-sufficient; they have their own religious schools, halls of worship, social and religious programs, and often host events such as interfaith services which are of communal importance. Most congregations have men's clubs and women's clubs, Parent-Teacher Associations, young people's leagues, senior citizen programs, adult study lectures and seminars, and, of course, a full cycle of religious activity. Membership in such congregations is normally requisite for participation in many or all of these activities. Every congregation, however, provides for families who are interested in its program but who are unable to meet the financial obligations that are attendant to normal membership.

Members of a congregation normally elect their board, and either the congregation as a whole or its board then elects the rabbi. Serving a congregation with many internal organizations and programmatic needs is not an easy task. It is a constant challenge to the rabbi and those who are associated with him: his assistant, if his congregation is large; the cantor; the principal of the school; the executive director; the boards and committees of the congregation. All must work together as a team, to carry out the avowed program of a particular temple.

It is evident that the rabbi must be the spiritual force giving direction to the various facets of Jewish congregational life, if it is to be permeated with the ideals of Judaism. This often puts the rabbi on a hectic treadmill of activities but there is hardly a calling in the world which demands so much of a man and, in turn, gives so much back in deep satisfaction. That is not to say that the rabbi is free of frustration. Because he wants to do so much and finds that the wheels of progress grind so exceedingly slowly, the aims which are clear in his mind tend to be overly long-delayed in their transmission to actuality. It has become part of the rabbi's duty to teach and convince others of the rightness of his position, and this is an inevitable part of his work.

The rabbis, who have always been the *avant garde* of Judaism and the molders of the tradition according to the needs of the times, are logically the first ones exposed to the winds of change. As Jewish life undergoes transformations, so does the rabbinate. To the question of "What is a rabbi?" it might then be proper to answer that he is a virtuoso of Judaism, whose artistry compels him at one time to play heavily on one string of faith while pressing lightly against the others, until the proper tune emerges —harmonious and fitting. Themes that were major in one generation become minor in another, and new themes have yet to be created. It is for this role that the rabbi has been chosen by the instrumentalities of Jewish history and Jewish destiny. It is to these two, then, that he must expertly respond.

### THE RABBI AS A TEACHER OF JUDAISM: PRIEST, PROPHET OR SAGE?

Rabbi Jacob Shankman recently observed in a fascinating essay, "The Changing Role of the Rabbi," that the inevitable substratum of the rabbinate is scholarship and teaching. Rabbi Shankman observes that the modern rabbi must at least be "a Jewish book-man familiar with the rich treasures of contemporary scholarly research and even aspire to make one specific area of study and learning his own." It is not uncommon to find in the rabbinate men who have specialized in philosophy, psychology, sociology, family counseling, and a host of other intellectual and vocational interests, all of which they seek to integrate into their traditional calling and learning. Because of the nature of American religious life, the rabbi teaches not only his congregation but often is invited to speak to other groups about Judaism. He accepts invitations to address Christian congregations and to lecture on campuses throughout the United States, to Jewish and non-Jewish college students. He must be prepared to present an intellectual exposition of Judaism to the Christian clergy which is most anxious to know of the antecedents of Christianity and which views the rabbi as expert in this area.

While the subject matter which the contemporary American rabbi must attempt to translate into a meaningful reality is different from that of his medieval and ancient counterpart, we can see that the function of the institution of the rabbinate remains the same. It has as its primary obligation the teaching and the interpretation of Judaism to Jews and to the world. It continues to be a hard but creative struggle. Judaism champions the quest rather than the pat answer to the complex problems of life and knowledge.

The rabbi, because he is expected to be a pastor and counselor to his congregation, has to know something of psychology and of group dynamics. As early as 1890, at the first annual convention of the Central Conference of American Rabbis in Cleveland, a rabbi saw as a new feature of the modern rabbinate the need to visit his congregants in an attempt to get to know them and their personal needs. It was not without a struggle that the rabbis accepted this particular function of the rabbinate. In recent years it has grown to almost unmanageable proportions and resulted, as Rabbi Robert Gordis observed, in a sort of topsy-turvy reversal of the rabbinic roles. "Instead of the rabbi being the scholar and the teacher *par excellence,* with few peripheral functions, his scholarship became secondary, or less than that, and his peripheral functions became central, and these in turn proliferated into a vast complex of activities."

It soon became apparent that the field of counseling required as much expertise in its own way as had the proper expounding of Jewish lore in a previous period. As more and more people brought their problems to the rabbi, he felt obliged to make himself conversant with community resources to which troubled people might turn for help. He became, and is, more of a specialist in referral than a psychotherapist or psychiatric social worker. Although there have been a number of rabbis who have specialized in this field and earned their doctorates in these areas, their pulpit work and their other congregational obligations prevent them from becoming full-time counselors within the congregation itself. Given the fact that the congregant turns to the rabbi, this particular function of the modern rabbinate is emerging as a matter of legitimate concern. The rabbi must know something about the nature of modern psychiatric techniques and therapies.

The modern rabbi also finds himself in the role of organizer and administrator. In the 1930's, the largest congregations in America had memberships of 500 to 800 families, with very few over 1,000. In 1966, there are a dozen congregations which exceed 1,500 families and some exceeding 2,500. Of course, the rabbis of such congregations usually have one or more assistants. The larger the congregation, the greater are the administrative and organizational problems, to say nothing of the great demands made upon the rabbi's time for pastoral counseling, teaching, and lecturing. As much as the rabbi might seek to avoid administrative and organizational problems, if he is at all conscientious he will find himself involved in decision-making previously unknown to the rabbinate. For example, the rabbi must have some understanding of how a budget is created and administered; he must be zealous of the allocations for his religious program and constantly alert to the danger of proliferation of activity extraneous to the religious program of his congregation.

The increasing number of vital communal needs, both local and national, also concern the rabbi. There is hardly a worthy cause in the United States, and in many instances abroad, that does not seek the rabbi's attention and support. These may range from human rights to the establishment of children's villages in Israel, from the rescuing of Jews in countries where Jewish existence is hazardous to a new *mikveh* that some rabbi wishes to build. The rabbi must choose, from among all the demands made upon him, those which are paramount in importance.

The rabbi is expected to be involved, and can be particularly potent, in local causes. The boards of the hospitals, symphony, public library, and even colleges and universities may turn to him for assistance. Because these causes are worth-while and members of his congregation benefit from them, the rabbi must seek to strengthen the social and cultural institutions which uplift the life of his community. For similar reasons, the rabbi may find it necessary to speak out prophetically against local, national, and international conditions which betray human inequality and which are injurious to the perpetuation of Judaism and of the Jewish people. The rabbi is expected to take an interest in developments in the state of Israel, particularly as they affect Jewry in America and the rest of the world. Far from being a marriage and burial clerk, a master of ceremonies, or joiner, the rabbi represents a positive social and communal force and is a central figure in the Jewish community.

As American Jewry continues to move forward, the rabbinate will grow in even greater significance. To meet these new challenges, the rabbi would do well to remain true to his calling—a perpetual student of Judaism but at home in the intellectual climate of the modern world. By integrating in his person the ancient roles of sage, priest, and prophet, he should develop his gifts as preacher, teacher, and counselor to convey his message forcefully and honestly. Amid his complex duties and responsibilities, the rabbi faces his moments of truth, realizing that he cannot do everything equally well. He therefore sharpens the tool of his rabbinate in specific functions, be it preaching, teaching, counseling, or communal work, and learns to do those phases of his work with great expertise and resourcefulness. Any young man with the prerequisite verbal and intellectual gifts, who has a deep love for his people and his religion, can be a rabbi.

## Should a Woman Be a Rabbi?

It has been asked occasionally, and debated on the floor of at least one rabbinic association, whether women should seek to become rabbis. There have been instances in which some women, few in number to be sure, have finished the rabbinic curriculum at one or another of the liberal seminaries but were not ordained. I, personally, knew of one young lady who had persuaded the Admissions Committee of the Hebrew Union College to admit her as a rabbinic candidate. She had the prerequisite Hebrew knowledge and seemed to be of fine character and background.

All of us students were anxiously awaiting the day of her ordination to test that which had been heretofore untried in Jewish life—a "woman rabbi." It developed, however, after a year or so of study, that the young lady was much more interested in becoming a *rebbitzen* (a rabbi's wife) than a rabbi. She stopped her studies after her wedding day, having succeeded in marrying a husband of her chosen profession.

The Reform movement seems to be the only available vehicle to a young woman who wishes to qualify for ordination as a rabbi. The Central Conference of American Rabbis has studied the question, and the Study Committee report made in 1956 recommended that educationally and spiritually qualified "female rabbinical students" be admitted to the Hebrew Union College-Jewish Institute of Religion. The school may endorse for ordination any woman who satisfactorily completes the required course leading to ordination.

It has been the position of the Reform movement from the very outset to grant equality of status to women in religious life and practice. It was only a logical extension of that principle that led to the Committee's resolution. It is of interest to note that the Rabbinical Assembly of America, in 1955, representing the Conservative viewpoint, permitted women to take part in leading the ritual in synagogue worship. It is not likely that the Conservative rabbinate will so readily move in the direction of the Central Conference of American Rabbis to grant endorsement for women to enter the rabbinate. Neither the Orthodox nor Conservative movement seem hospitable even to the idea of such a "happening."

A number of rabbis commented at the time that these deliberations were taking place, as reported in the *Jewish Digest* of May, 1957. I believe these comments are a barometer of opinion within each movement. Dr. Oscar Z. Fasman, president of the Hebrew Theological College, an Orthodox seminary near Chicago, categorically said, "No" on the ground that "no *halakhah* so teaches." Rabbi Abraham J. Feldman (Reform) stated, "If women ask to be ordained as rabbis and accept the discipline and training, study and preparation required of male rabbis, I see no reason why such ordination should be denied to them."

Rabbi Sidney E. Hoenig, a professor at Yeshiva University (Orthodox), elaborated the position espoused by Rabbi Fasman.

> Jewish tradition, as enunciated in the Talmud and Codes, recognizes that, because of their physical constitution, women are not obligated to observe many of the "positive commandments" of the Law. Since they have no "obligation of observance," they cannot act as agents, or proxies, or fulfill obligations for others. Hence they cannot decide any *halakic* matters, serve as *dayyan* or as a member of a *Beth Din* (law court), which *Semicha,* the traditional rabbinic ordination, implies. Nor can they lead others in prayer or direct communities in observance of Jewish practice from which they themselves are excused.

Rabbi Hoenig hastens to add that "the advice and guidance of women in the practice of Jewish law is not ignored," but "an official position . . . as rabbi has never been given to a woman, and Orthodoxy will uphold that traditional line."

It is a matter of record that at least three Jewish congregations, two on this continent and one in England, have had spiritual leaders who were women, unordained. Lady Lily Montagu was such a "minister" of the West Central Jewish Liberal Congregation in London. An outstanding personality in Reform Jewish life in Great Britain, she has made, particularly through her work in the establishment of the World Union for Progressive Judaism, an historic contribution to the development of liberal Judaism in Europe. The Society of Jewish Science of New York, founded by the late Rabbi Morris Lichtenstein, has had his widow as its leader since 1940. Both daughter and sister-in-law of Orthodox rabbis, Mrs. Lichtenstein has continued a movement which is akin to Christian Science. Another instance of a rabbi's widow succeeding him in the pulpit was Mrs. William

Ackerman of Meridian, Mississippi, who was elected as the congregation's spiritual leader and served until 1955.

Lady Montagu observed, as quoted in the *Jewish Digest:*

From the practical point of view, we have to admit that today few congregations would accept the spiritual leadership of a woman if a man were available. So candidates dependent on this work for a living would have to hesitate before accepting the training even when freely offered to them. But prejudice is removed by time. There is little doubt that if women are prepared to recognize that their ministry must depend on the development of their full intellectual powers, as well as those of heart and spirit, they will, before long, see their services eagerly accepted by the congregations.

The roles of mother and wife and the enormous responsibilities attendant to those roles will preclude the actuality of women entering the ordained rabbinate in large numbers. That there will be some in the future, there is no doubt.

## CHAPTER II

# My Religious Commitment

## SHOULD AN ATHEIST OR AGNOSTIC CONSIDER THE RABBINATE?

Since one of the cardinal principles of Judaism is the belief · in the existence of God, an atheist should obviously preclude himself from choosing the rabbinate as a career. Since, in the congregational rabbinate particularly, the rabbi officiates at religious services in which the reading of prayers is central, it would be an act of the utmost hypocrisy for an atheist to see himself as honestly functioning in this role. The rabbi who is the representative of religious Judaism must have a deep and abiding faith in God. The rabbi's concept of God may grow with his experiences and studies; his God concepts may change radically or slightly. But the rabbi must have a profound belief in something greater than himself which gives meaning and purpose to life, and which he deems vital and animating to all that exists. As the bedrock of his faith, the rabbi's idea of God gives shape to all of the other beliefs and acts of his rabbinate.

Judaism's God concepts have grown to maturity in its long history. Despite its diversity of approaches to gaining knowledge of God, whether rational, mystical, or existential, some basic beliefs have remained characteristic of it. Judaism is a religion which teaches that God is One, that He is a unity in which all else finds its being. In addition, there is an ethical side to God to which man responds and which, in turn, responds to man. This religious philosophy is called ethical monotheism. Judaism envisages man and God as partners in the process of continuous creation; there is an interdependence of man and God in bringing about the rectification of the world. The Jew is aware of his dependence upon God and he knows that the fulfillment of God's plan for man, as envisaged in the Torah, depends on his living a life of *mitzvot*. Judaism also teaches that Israel received a unique revelation of God's nature. Orthodoxy holds that this revelation took place at one breakthrough in human consciousness at Mt. Sinai, with the giving of the Ten Commandments and the Torah. Conservatism and Reform maintain that Israel's revelation is on-going. Israel saw God in every moment of its history and not only at Sinai. This special awareness of God's mandates for man makes of Israel a "special people" (*am segulah*), whose task it is to live the truths of its vision and to teach them to other men. Reform Judaism has called this the "mission of Israel" and points to this prophetic function as the chief reason for the necessary and continued existence of Judaism. A Jewish atheist, who would argue that the teachings of ethical monotheism and its corollary principles are "dead," is obviously misplaced in the rabbinate.

It is somewhat different with the young person who is an agnostic. It was T. H. Huxley who first spoke of "agnostics." He contrasted his knowledge of God with that of the Gnostics of the ancient world who claimed to have a special *gnosis* (knowledge) of God's nature. An *a-gnostic,* as Huxley taught, is someone who has no absolute, irrefutable knowledge of God. While *gnosis,* for the Orthodox group, might equal the revealed Torah at Sinai, which for them is absolute, this is not the case with Reform or Conservative Judaism. Since God continues to exist, *gnosis* of him is not frozen, nor is truth concerning him bound securely in a book or series of books. The great medieval Jewish philosopher Maimonides (1135-1204 C.E.), when faced with the problem of defining God, would only say what God was not. He full well understood that defining God in absolute language limits our conception of him. This was a form of agnosticism but within the general framework of the ongoing body of Jewish belief. I consider this type of Jewish agnosticism among the most serious of *religious* positions and intellectual commitments. In many ways agnosticism corresponds to the major tendency of Jewish speculative thought since Maimonides. I have reference to the agnosticism which is convinced of the existence of some superior power, something which transcends man and through which man finds his being, but concerning the full nature of which knowledge is incomplete. It has been a cardinal principle of most Jewish philosophers, with few exceptions, not to close the discussion on theological issues, including the question of God's nature. Jewish philosophers realized that once they made a positive definition of God, subsequent new knowledge and experience would make it difficult to change a fixed concept.

Orthodox Judaism would take issue with the particular viewpoint just described, and would maintain that to be an Orthodox rabbi, only the accepted traditional God concept could qualify one as a rabbinic candidate. In the Orthodox position, God is supernatural. It is only such a God that can command man, and it is only to such a God that man can respond through prayer. Reform Judaism and the Liberal wing of Conservative Judaism would be hospitable to the other expressions as well, of one's ideas of God.

It is my conviction that a young man seriously in search of God and unsure as yet of his full understanding of Him, may consider himself a candidate for the rabbinate. He must, however, choose a seminary in which his quest will not be misunderstood as basic doubt.

## WHERE DO I STAND?

### 1. *Am I Orthodox?*

It is likely that if you are Orthodox, you know it. An Orthodox Jew scrupulously observes *halakhah*. This involves strict adherence to Jewish law and a host of customs that make up the life of the fully observant Jew. It is usual for the candidate for the Orthodox rabbinate to be a graduate of a Jewish parochial elementary school and high school known as a *yeshiva*. On occasion, there are candidates for the Orthodox rabbinate who come from nonreligious homes or from the other branches of

Judaism. In such instances, the candidate must somehow master the required traditional background materials. There are also other qualifications necessary to be considered Orthodox which relate to theological beliefs and life attitudes.

The spectrum of affiliation in Orthodoxy is quite varied, and much depends upon whether one is ultra-Orthodox or modern Orthodox. The *Hasidic* groups would fall into the first category, while "Young Israel" might aptly fit the second. The ultra-Orthodox might well consider a member of Young Israel or a Yeshiva University graduate as a reformer. Within the Orthodox community, then, there is a right and a left wing as well as an ever-growing center which seeks to moderate divergent opinions. One will find this divergence of viewpoint reflected in the large net of day schools which feed the Orthodox seminaries their rabbinic candidates. There are presently some 56,000 pupils in about 300 Orthodox day schools under various sponsorships, in the United States and Canada.

There are variations in viewpoint and custom among the Orthodox synagogues. For example, the *shtibl*-type synagogues, meeting in small rooms in which the vocal participation of the congregants defies any modicum of decorum; and the modern Orthodox synagogue, where one hears the service conducted by a capable cantor with a trained voice, using mechanical acoustical equipment. The ultra-Orthodox synagogue separates men from women during worship, either by a partition through the middle of the synagogue or by a women's gallery. There are modern Orthodox synagogues where men and women are seated together, and where one finds decorum.

The term "Orthodox" is derived from the combination of two Greek words, *ortho,* meaning right or proper, and *doxa,* meaning opinion. The term was first employed by Abraham Furtado, president of the Sanhedrin convoked by Napoleon, in Paris, in the year 1807. The term has more often been used as a descriptive one by those who are non-Orthodox, although today it is employed by many traditionalists to describe their system of practice and belief. Many Orthodox Jews prefer a different desig-

nation, such as "*Torah*-true Jews," or, as those who believe in
"*Torah im Derekh Eretz,*" meaning Torah together with secular
knowledge. Rabbi Emanuel Rackman, a leading Orthodox
thinker, makes the following observation:

Notwithstanding popular opinion to the contrary, Orthodox
Judaism does not give its adherents unequivocal answers to
the basic questions of life. Nor does it even prescribe for every
situation in which the Jew may find himself. What it does
have is religious, philosophical and ethical imperatives; these
are often antithetical in character and man is rarely spared
the onus of deliberate choice and decision. It is important to
point this out for the benefit of those who are already committed to the Law as well as for those who are about to
embrace it.

Rabbi Rackman points out that "Judaism affords no escape from
the awareness of reality or the exercise of reason. Indeed, the
divinely revealed must be true—in the absolute sense—and what
is absolutely true can be an anchor for emotional and intellectual
security." That this position of the modern Orthodox movement
is far from secured can be measured by the remarks of Professor
Leon Stitskin of Yeshiva University. Addressing himself to the
ultratraditionalist wing of his movement, he observed:

There are those who would oppose a synthesis of Torah
values with general knowledge (*Torah* and *Mada*) for fear
of diluting the former. Yeshiva University has pursued a
policy of blending the eternal verities of Torah with academic
learning in order to develop a fully integrated personality.
    Our Torah does not need to be sheltered or protected. Its
abiding values are not only capable of withstanding the
exigencies of surrounding cultures, but can help mold and
humanize them. The impact of Torah verities are everlastingly
meaningful and challenging.

In order to consider oneself Orthodox, there are certain cardinal principles, as well as religious modes of conduct, to which allegiance must be given. Rabbi Leo Jung, a foremost Orthodox scholar, maintains:

> The one doctrine whence all arises is that of revelation
> . . . what had been conveyed by Torah is not the fruit of Moses' genius nor the summing-up or re-statement of the wisdom or insights of many, but the uncovering (that is what "reveal" means) of the nature of God and His role in the affairs of the cosmos and of men. The revelation of Sinai yielded the doctrine that God by His nature is unique and absolute. He is Law-giver and the Torah provides the vehicle whereby man can endeavor to imitate Him and His qualities of righteousness and mercy. It is necessary, therfeore, to accept the Torah as a set of principles, a body of practice, as a faith and an attitude requiring "study as a method of worship" and "worship as a method of study." This is to lead to ethical consciousness and create the striving for a more perfect society. The Torah contains certain precepts grounded in the Five Books of Moses, supplemented by the teaching of the prophets, and the application of these teachings by the rabbis in an uninterrupted chain of activity spanning Judaism's history and "forming the skeleton of the national building." This complex of legal tradition shapes the *halakhah* which is the Jewish way of life and which, based on its classic texts, is made applicable by certain prescribed procedures of interpretation to the new conditions in which the Jew finds himself.

It is a cardinal principle of Orthodoxy, and herein it differs from Reform Judaism perceptibly, that no Jew can lawfully put his own interpretation on *halakhah* according to his own insights and understanding of *halakhah*. This doctrine of revelation is the bedrock upon which Orthodoxy rests and from which its other facets of interpretation are derived. If you are an Orthodox

Jew you believe that "*Torah*-true Judaism" is life and law which provides training and character and induces a total world view. Certain duties between God and man, between man and man, ensue from this understanding of revelation. Among many laws and traditions, the Orthodox Jew is expected to adhere strictly to the dietary laws, the laws pertaining to the observance of the Sabbath and the holidays, the covering of the head at all times, daily worship, the wearing of phylacteries for the morning services, with exceptions as the Law provides, and the wearing of *tzitzit,* a garment with fringes to bring one to the constant awareness of the presence of God in one's life.

The written law and the oral law represent the compendium of Jewish law and life and are to be understood in their fundamental essence. Higher criticism of the Bible, which would tend to show that the Five Books of Moses represents a collection of documents spanning a thousand years of creativity, would be precluded as a vehicle of understanding Jewish tradition. Orthodoxy, then, is as much a psychology as a philosophy of life. An individual who is committed to the many precepts of Jewish law, and is willing to live these, may consider himself and be considered by others as an Orthodox Jew.

## 2. Am I a Reform Jew?

Reform Judaism is the vigorous and dynamic faith which first attempted to reconcile Judaism with the modern world. Reform claims one million adherents on the American continent and is the oldest organized religious movement in America. While the roots of Reform Judaism go back to the beginning of the nineteenth century in Germany, the movement grew to maturity and its greatest flowering in America. The brilliant organizing genius of Isaac Mayer Wise established the Union of American Hebrew Congregations in Cincinnati, Ohio, in 1873. Its purpose, as stated in its constitution, is "to encourage and aid the organization and development of Jewish congregations; to promote Jewish education and enrich and intensify Jewish life; to maintain the Hebrew Union College-Jewish Institute of Religion; and to foster other activities for the perpetuation and advancement of Judaism." In 1875 Wise founded the Hebrew Union College, whose purpose was to train rabbis nurtured on American soil. Wise was the first to see that if Judaism in America was to have a future, it needed to be sustained by American Jews and could no longer rely upon European religious leadership. Little did Wise, or any of his contemporaries, realize how fateful such a prediction would be. With the decimation of the great centers of European Jewry during the Nazi era, America emerged as the greatest center of Jewish life and learning in the world.

Wise, from the outset, was interested in creating a *"Minhag-America"*; that is, an American way of living a Jewish life. His original attempts were directed at unifying the rabbinate and congregations in America. His vision was grand but the realities of the situation mitigated against its fulfillment. Wise founded the Central Conference of American Rabbis, in 1889. Contrary to popular opinion, Reform Judaism has never been of only one religious viewpoint. While it has adopted two platforms of belief —one in 1885 known as the Pittsburgh Platform, the other in 1937 known as the Columbus Platform—Reform Judaism has remained alive to the theological and social currents of America and the world. If there has been a single characteristic of Reform Judaism, it has been its impatience with the status quo. Recently Rabbi Maurice N. Eisendrath, the president of the Union of American Hebrew Congregations, expressed this view most extremely when he urged his colleagues of the Central Conference of American Rabbis "to be candid enough to confess that a new, more revolutionary Reform Judaism is needed" and that "otherwise we are frozen in a neo-Orthodoxy."

Whereas the Orthodox movement emphasizes *"Torah*-true Judaism," and Conservative Judaism, in the words of Solomon Schechter, extolls "Law-mindedness" in the rabbi, the Reform movement underscores the rabbi and his prophetic tradition. The Reform movement is always attempting to develop new forms of expression for Judaism's ancient faith, creed, and ritual. It was in the nature of the early reformers to be drastic in their attempt to strip Judaism of seemingly irrelevant externalities which, like the husk on a cob of corn, concealed its kernel. It was the viewpoint of the Reform movement that Judaism could not survive in the modern world in its ancient ghetto garb. On the other hand, Reform attempted to critically understand the history and evolution of Jewish religious thought and practice. Its rabbis were pioneers in what has been called "the science of Judaism." Through scholarly inquiry into Israel's ancient past, it was discovered that Judaism in its biblical and talmudic period was a vital religion, creating new concepts and practices from within as time and circumstance required.

Reform Judaism's concept of revelation reflected the belief that revelation was not frozen to one moment of history on Sinai but was an on-going process in which each generation participated and in which each generation found its own truths. Because Reform Judaism was born in the Age of Enlightenment, which relied heavily on man's reason, it was believed that revelation was progressive and that each generation could stand on the shoulders of its predecessors to see newer and greater truths for Israel and all of mankind. It was therefore incumbent upon Reform Judaism to attempt to reconcile Jewish belief with modern thought and to welcome all truth, whether ancient or modern. Wise taught: "Judaism . . . maintains that God is no less revealed in nature and history than in the Bible, and His operations must be observed and His perfection studied in all departments of revelation."

The temper of Reform Judaism insisted upon a rational faith for the modern Jew. In its eagerness to make Judaism once again credible, it removed much from the area of ceremony which seemed a hindrance to this quest. Rabbi Solomon Freehof has observed that early Reform Judaism

. . . considered the ceremonial system to be a trivializing of the noble teaching of Judaism. Even the deep learning involved in the study of it was looked upon as a wastage of intellectual capacity, an alienation of the broader culture of the modern world. This anti-ritual attitude seemed to be confirmed by events in Orthodoxy itself, for in wider and wider Orthodox circles the very spiritual basis of the old ritual rapidly seeped away. Fewer and fewer children of Israel continued to believe that these observances had come to us as a genuine mandate from God. As long as Jews did believe that, as they did for centuries, then all of each day's ritual was truly a pageant dedicated to the Omnipresent, but once they ceased to believe that, it did become mere routine and blind piety.

It was for this reason that the Reform movement sought compatibility with new thought rather than with tradition. The pioneer Reform Rabbi Abraham Geiger's motto was: "To search in the past, to live in the present, to build for the future." It is that credo which Reform Judaism has attempted to hold firmly before its inner eye.

The advocates of Reform in Germany revised the traditional prayer book, putting much of the liturgy in the vernacular and excluding from it ritual and ideas they believed to be outmoded. The ceremony of Bar Mitzvah, which had become routinized, was supplemented by the Confirmation. It was first introduced for boys and then also expanded to include girls. Despite great opposition to it, the ceremony rapidly became popular and was adopted by many congregations whose ritual was otherwise according to tradition. The inclusion of girls in Confirmation came to symbolize the equality of women in religion and their importance in the perpetuation of Jewish life. The reformers eliminated the women's gallery as well as the whole mentality which made of women second-class religious citizens. Reform Judaism returned to the biblical calendar in its scheduling of the festivals and of the New Year. It rejected the mind-set that made credibility in miracles mandatory. It removed the obligatory character of the dietary laws, as well as the notion of the resurrection of the body after death. Reform emphasized the need to observe

the Sabbath and the Holy Days but made room for contemporary
interpretation of the festivals and life-cycle ceremonies of the
Jew.

Because Reform Judaism was born in a century of unbridled
hope in the capacity of man to better his condition, the notion
of "a messianic era" instead of faith in a personal messiah was
advocated, particularly by Abraham Geiger. This was viewed as
an age in which there was to be universal righteousness, brotherhood, and peace. It was, in fact, an ideal which had originally
been voiced by the prophets of ancient Israel and had also been
taught by the rabbis of the talmudic era. Reform Judaism made
much of the prophetic teaching that Israel was God's elected
people and had a universal mission in the world. It is for this
reason that a return to Palestine was negated in early Reform
theology and anti-Zionist elements included in its formulations.

A change in viewpoint on Zionism was brought about and
incorporated into the Columbus Platform of 1937. It reads:

> In all lands where our people live, they assume and seek
> to share loyally the full duties and responsibilities of citizen-
> ship and to create seats of knowledge and religion. In the
> rehabilitation of Palestine, a land hallowed by memories and
> hopes, we behold the promise of renewed life for many of our
> brethren. We affirm the obligation of all Jewry to aid in its
> upbuilding as a Jewish homeland by endeavoring to make it
> not only to be a haven of refuge for the oppressed but also a
> center of Jewish culture and spiritual life.

The sentiment of the Central Conference of American Rabbis
is today preponderantly in favor of some type of Zionist philosophy.

Reform Judaism's commitment to the prophetic ideal of social
justice led it from the very outset to pioneer in social action.
The Columbus Platform's plea that "Judaism seeks the attainment of a just society by the application of its teachings through
the economic order, industry and commerce, and through na-

tional and international affairs" propelled the members of the
Conference into the eye of the hurricane of social change. While
it is common today to see rabbis of all branches of Judaism involved in social action, this was not always the case. Reform
rabbis were pace-setters among the Jewish clergy in attempting
to extend the doctrines of prophetic teaching into the lifeblood
of society. Rabbi Stephen S. Wise, the founder of the Jewish
Institute of Religion, a dynamic and magnetic leader and organizer, was perhaps foremost an exemplar of the prophetic tradition. The Union of American Hebrew Congregations' Religious
Action Center in Washington is the first, and presently the only,
such establishment in American Jewish religious life, dramatizing
to the nation that Jews are concerned with the moral issues of
legislation, in the rightness of the law, as well as in its efficacy.

The candidate who aspires to the Reform rabbinate must have
a hunger for a deep knowledge of the ideas of Judaism. He
must also know the world in which he lives, intimately and in a
far-reaching way. He must have an "informed kind of *emunah*,"
an enlightened faith. Dr. Nelson Glueck, president of the con-
joined Hebrew Union College-Jewish Institute of Religion, a
great scholar and archeologist, observes:

> Reform Judaism is often misunderstood and misrepresented
> as being minimal in its demands. In its truest definition, it has
> ever insisted not upon less dedication, less information, less
> observance, but upon richer understanding of, and warmer
> devotion to, the fundamentals of our faith. Reform Judaism
> remains, and has always been concerned with the totality of
> all of Israel, in whose destiny it is intertwined and in whose
> hope it sees its brightest future.

### 3. *Do I Belong With the Conservatives?*

The hub of the Conservative movement in the Western
Hemisphere is the Jewish Theological Seminary of America,
located in New York and presided over by Dr. Louis Finkelstein.
The Jewish Theological Seminary came into being as a reaction

against the liberality of the Reform movement, as expressed in the Pittsburgh Platform of 1885. In this Platform, Reform Judaism asserted itself primarily as a religious group, denying the implications of nationhood and the aspiration to restore the Jewish national home in Palestine. It also severed, in principle, the binding power of Jewish traditional law and dropped many observances which had come to permeate Jewish life. Disturbed by these breaks with traditional Judaism, a small group of English-speaking rabbis decided to form a theological seminary which would oppose these tendencies and which would act as a counterbalance to the Hebrew Union College. The Jewish Theological Seminary opened in 1887, and in 1902 the distinguished Rabbi Solomon Schechter, who was a Reader in Rabbinics at Cambridge University, was invited to become its president. This exemplary scholar and administrator guided this institution to a place of great prominence, where it became the primary exponent of what is called Conservative Judaism.

From the outset, and for a long time thereafter, the religious leaders of the Seminary made no attempt to create a new movement or to follow the precedent set by the Central Conference of American Rabbis in framing a platform of common beliefs. The Seminary's slogan was "catholic Israel" and appealed to a segment of Jews for whom Reform Judaism was too radical and Orthodoxy too traditional. The bulk of its supporters came from Eastern European Jewry, especially Jews of Poland, Russia, Hungary, and Rumania. The Conservatives refused to articulate a systematic program and were often attacked by the Orthodox as being a timid Reform. The formulators of the Conservative position, particularly Dr. Schechter, followed a pragmatic approach in their attempt to weave an American Judaism for traditionalists who wanted to live a Jewish life within their American environment. The architects of Conservatism drew together a consensus of viewpoints which still operates today.

Reaching back to the platform of the Theological Seminary in Breslau, and the ideas of its intellectual leader, Zacharias Frankel, Conservative Judaism expounded the position of "posi-

tive-historical Judaism." Frankel hoped to indicate by this unusual designation the process of change within traditional Judaism. He championed the view that Judaism is the product of
historical development. Frankel held it to be wrong, for the
sake of comprehension of the liturgy, to surrender the primacy
of the Hebrew language in worship. Frankel defended many
other traditional beliefs but insisted also on the need for scientific research. Since Judaism is the product of an evolutionary
process, an attempt must be made to understand its growth and
development. Frankel also underscored the importance of the
national elements in Judaism which Rabbi Solomon Schechter
later used in his own formulation of the idea of "religious nation-
alism."

Ahad Ha-Am, a philosopher and essayist (1856-1927), who
was born in Russia and died in Palestine, developed the viewpoint that Judaism has a culture as well as a religion. He was
the architect of the philosophy which came to be known as
"Cultural Zionism," in which Palestine was viewed as the spiritual center of the Jewish people. Renewed cultural activity and
the re-creation of Hebrew language and literature could most
naturally take place there. He also emphasized the ethical character of Judaism. Utilizing this approach, a disciple of his, Professor Israel Friedlander (1876-1920), a faculty member of the
Jewish Theological Seminary, developed the position that Judaism is a complete culture and not merely a creed. Professor Louis
Ginzberg, a great talmudic scholar, continued in the tradition of
Frankel to develop critical methods of studying rabbinic literature and law. He stressed the need to interpret the ideas and
practices of Jewish tradition.

Professor Mordecai M. Kaplan enlarged upon these ideas and
founded the Reconstructionist movement. Reconstructionism
was meant to be a pervasive philosophy of Jewish life, whose
teachings could be inserted into the other movements. Practically
speaking, this has taken place only within the Conservative and
Reform movements. Reconstructionists have no seminary of
their own, which is why, perhaps, the movement has not grown

perceptibly of late. Reconstructionism is a Jewish humanist philosophy in which Judaism is viewed as a religious civilization. A civilization implies a cultural and linguistic content, and is concerned with the totality of existence. Reconstructionism has accented long-neglected facets of Jewish culture, such as music and art, which at one time were part and parcel of a full Jewish life. The Reconstructionist philosophy stresses the importance of cultural forms in shaping the identity of the modern Jew, such as the rebirth of Hebrew as a spoken tongue and as a source for new creativity. Judaism, which is seen as an evolving religious civilization of the Jewish people, features the people as the central factor of Jewish experience. Dr. Kaplan has focused upon the nature of Jewish peoplehood, which is also the bearer of the Jewish civilizational mold.

On the question of the nature of God, Dr. Kaplan believes that ancient nomenclature is no longer valid. For him, God is process in which the cosmic principle of polarity operates. Subjectively, God is experienced as that power within us which makes us redeem our society and our human condition. This power leads us to concretize Jewish ethical norms into daily experience. In his view of God, Kaplan is far removed from the official positions of both the Conservative and Reform movements, and yet, paradoxically, enjoys an influential following of both Conservative and Reform rabbis who have embraced this theology.

If one comes to the decision to be a rabbi because of convictions that Reconstructionism holds much truth, the Conservative and Reform seminaries lend a more hospitable atmosphere to candidates of this persuasion.

There are some basic requirements which the Seminary demands of its applicants for the rabbinate. Observance of the dietary laws, the Sabbath and festivals, daily prayers, and conduct according to Jewish law and tradition. Rabbi Robert Gordis capsules the basic philosophy of Conservative Judaism as follows: "Judaism is the evolving religious culture and civilization of the Jewish people." The practical implications of this point of view have made Conservative Judaism adaptive to its American environment and has been able to make the program of Conservative Judaism flexible. It is becoming increasingly more difficult to differentiate between a traditional minded Reform Jew and a liberally oriented Conservative Jew. Conservatives have accepted mixed seating at worship services, and many other practices which had previously been labeled "Reform." The services are conducted in English and in Hebrew, and the average sermon topic of the Conservative rabbi is closely akin to that of his Reform counterpart. Basically, what still differentiates the Conservative and the Reform Jew, aside from the institutional commitments which exist, are a temper of mind regarding the uses of tradition, law, and the obligatory nature of some observance.

Among the Conservative rabbis I have known, I have found internal differences on many theological issues. There are some Conservative rabbis whose ideology is more radical than that of some Reform rabbis, and some Reform rabbis whose theology is much more traditional than that of some Conservative rabbis. In time, a reappraisal of the respective positions of the Conservative and Reform movements will undoubtedly have to be made, and perhaps a real rapprochement of many Conservative and Reform rabbis can be effected.

The key issue separating Conservative and Reform rabbis is the binding authority of *halakhah*. The Conservative movement has loosened the thread of *halakhah* considerably so as to become vulnerable in the eyes of the Orthodox. On the other hand, Reform rabbis, having broken with the binding nature of *halakhah* altogether, often find the position of Conservative rabbis to be inconsistent. Rabbi Gordis has summarized the position of the Conservatives very well in his statement:

If we surrender our adherence to Jewish Law, we shall be courting anarchy; if we suffer it to petrify, we shall be inviting disaster. Our goal is loyalty to an evolving Law, which is the will of God as revealed through the experience of Israel.

If this statement represents your view on Jewish law and experience, and you adhere to otherwise traditional norms and practices, then you are indeed of the Conservative persuasion and should consider yourself a Conservative Jew.

## My Values and the Rabbinic Calling

Often, the religious rearing of childhood undergoes painstaking reappraisal as one grows to maturity, and the beliefs of one's youth suffer drastic revision. In conjunction with this appraisal of theological position must come the honest evaluation of values and whether these are in harmony with the rabbinic calling. More so than most callings, the rabbi himself, in his life and thought, represents the teaching of Judaism. The rabbis of the Mishnah observed, "Not learning but doing is the chief thing." The rabbi is judged more often by what he is and does than by what he knows. The talmudic sage Rabbah instructs us that "any rabbi whose inside is not like his outside is no rabbi." The revered Rabbi Leo Baeck taught: "The message is not the sermon of a preacher but the man himself. The man must be the message. The rabbi must not deliver a message, he must deliver himself."

One of the essential characteristics of the candidate for rabbinic study is that he must be an idealist. By this I do not mean to imply that he is required to be deaf to worldly demands or to his practical needs and those of his family. Asceticism is not an ideal of Judaism. Judaism expounds an indissoluble unity of body and soul, heart and mind. A rabbi's idealism must be a genuine part of his personality and not some accrued, belated affectation. One expresses oneself not only in synagogue or at stated times, but through the totality of every day of life. Because the rabbi must be an idealist, certain practical consequences flow from this position. The ancient rabbis implied by their teaching that the scholar of Torah, in order to achieve the maximum independence in his quest for truth, must reduce his material requirements to the absolute minimum. He should be prepared to sacrifice worldly goods for his integrity, should this be necessary. The rabbinic student who envisages the rabbinate as a vocation at which he can make sizeable amounts of money is sorely misguided. There are very few rabbis who remain in the rabbinate because of its material rewards. Because of the caliber of the average rabbi, he could do financially at least as well in some other vocation; the monetary reward is hardly an inducement to remain in a difficult and immensely challenging calling. The rabbi's primary incentive is his idealism.

Rabbi Abraham J. Feldman has highlighted two ideals which are, in his opinion, the indispensable minimum in the rabbinate, "To serve God and to serve his people Israel constitute the principal tasks of the rabbinate. All the other fascinations there are about this profession do not in themselves constitute a valid reason for entering it." Rabbi Feldman asked the question, why "serve Israel?" He answers that we start where the roots of Judaism are. We begin a structure by laying the foundations and gradually building upward. It is when we destroy a structure that demolition is started from the top and proceeds toward the foundations, as when a tree begins to die, it withers first at the top. In the constructive work of the rabbinate, the foundation is service to the people of Israel. While the rabbi is ordained by a particular movement, to be of specific service to it, his own concept of his calling must embrace service to the totality of Israel.

An ideal of the rabbi, without which service to his people is impossible, is a love and respect for fellow human beings. Far from lording it over a congregation or institution, a rabbi must be capable of entering into genuine dialogue with his congregants and associates. It must be remembered that, apart from the solitary hours the rabbi spends in his study in pursuit of knowledge, his work is with people for "life is with people." He conducts services, officiates at weddings and funerals, names and blesses new-born children, visits the sick and the bereaved, counsels the troubled, confers with those who seek his advice for important decisions in their lives, addresses gatherings, participates in dedications and a host of other congregational and communal

functions. A rabbi who dislikes people will be a miserable rabbi.
He will be tormented by the many hours that he must spend as a
public figure and the endless effort he must expend with others in
the day to day flow of his work.

The love of study must be part of the rabbi's system of values
and represent the bedrock upon which his preaching and lectures are based. A man who teaches but does not study will soon
be like an empty vessel, resounding with hollow echoes. Often
in the solitude of his study, among his books, new insights are
born and new dedication wells up, enabling the rabbi to be more
effective and creative. While the intellectual demands made upon
the rabbi may vary from congregation to congregation within
Judaism, it is becoming increasingly evident that the preponderant number of Jewish congregants are college graduates and
represent a wide spectrum of professional attainment. There is
hardly a congregation that does not have within it college professors, lawyers, doctors, aero-space technicians, physicists, as
well as many other representatives of emerging new professions.
The level of their education is graduate and postgraduate, and
the rabbi must attempt to reach this growing segment of his congregation through intellectually acceptable addresses and sermons. The rabbi is fortunate who will learn from his congregants
even while he teaches them.

The rabbi has to be a forceful person, capable of articulating
his thoughts with precision and conviction. There is a terrible
temptation in the rabbinate to hanker after meaningless popular-
ity and admiration. For this reason, I feel that a candidate for
the rabbinate must be essentially a modest man who will not seek
admirers but attempt to gain followers. While every rabbi is,
of course, human and imperfect, his sense of values must be such
as to counterbalance the vulgarities in contemporary life. His
absorption must be with the timeless and not only with the
timely, and this requires great courage. Rabbi Robert Hammer,
in an article, "Character-destroying Factors in the Rabbinate,"
observes:

The rabbinate is one of the world's most dangerous ways of life for it makes demands and imposes stresses that are both impossible and contradictory . . . The authority that he must assume endangers humility, the righteousness with which he must act is often too close to self-righteousness. The rabbinic character is distorted by these conflicting attitudes toward the rabbi. He is too freely criticized, but also too freely flattered; too fiercely possessed and too coldly deplored.

The rabbi must be very clear in his mind as to what he believes his principles to be, and with these he must never compromise. Neither adulation nor criticism should swerve him from what he knows to be right; this he must be willing to live and dramatize by his own teaching and conduct.

Another constellation of values revolves around the rabbi's basic world outlook. His primary concern is with leading a religious life imbued with Jewish faith and values. This requires a sense of inner piety, which should deepen through the years. The rabbi has to be willing and able to officiate at services and at the life-cycle ceremonies of his congregation. These cannot be merely perfunctory rites and rituals for him. Each occasion presents a new challenge to the rabbi and he needs to find within himself the capacity to make these events meaningful. The uninspired rabbi, the cold officiator, the marriage and burial clerk mentality reflects a rabbi who is devoid of personal piety, or who has lost the capacity to find religious meaning in the events which confront his daily life.

With these general values necessary to the rabbinic calling delineated, we might now establish an additional check-sheet of helpful attributes.

1. A rabbi must speak and write well. Words are his tools for imparting knowledge and, consequently, he must strive to master the techniques necessary for conveying his thoughts. I shall never forget the first sermon I submitted to my teacher of homiletics,

Dr. Israel Bettan, of blessed memory. Scrawled on the back of the sermon was the cryptic note, "See me!" With great trepidation, I went to see Dr. Bettan to hear his criticism. In his inimitable style, he commented on this or that passage and then finally he threw the caveat. "Your style, my friend, is so heavy and cumbersome. Why don't you write like this: 'The Lord is my shepherd, I shall not want'—crystal-clear!" I have never been able to forget Dr. Bettan's advice, either in the preparation of a sermon or of a manuscript. Whatever is imparted must be crystal-clear and this involves considerable effort.

2. The rabbinic candidate has to possess the capacity for empathy. Rabbi Robert Katz, Professor of Human Relations at the Hebrew Union College, states that "When we experience empathy we feel as if we are experiencing someone else's feeling as our own. We see, we feel, we respond, and we understand as if we were, in fact, the other person. We stand in his shoes. We get under his skin." In order for the rabbi to counsel and help others, he needs to understand the situation of the other person. Our sages put it this way: "Do not judge another person until you stand in his place." The capacity to feel empathy is vital to the rabbi.

3. Patience with the failings of others, and humility about one's own accomplishments or feelings of superiority, are very necessary. The rabbi who is a teacher knows that as a flower comes to blossom but slowly, so does understanding in the mind and heart of his pupil. It may take years to convince some members of a congregation as to the correctness of a cherished viewpoint. In the process, the rabbi must always work with awareness of his own fallibility, mindful that, indeed, the views of others may be more correct than his own.

4. A good heart is indispensable to the rabbinate. The great sage, Rabbi Jochanan ben Zakkai, once dispatched his disciples to go into the world and see what it was that a man should cherish the most. The disciples returned and gave their report. One said, "A generous eye." Another said, "A loyal friend." A third said, "A good neighbor." A fourth said, "The gift of

foresight." The last, Rabbi Elazar, said, "A good heart." It is reported that Rabbi Jochanan said, "I prefer the answer of Rabbi Elazar ben Arach to those of the rest of you, for in his words yours are included." In modern terms, having a good heart means being a good human being. The rabbi's own generosity and acts of goodness must rise spontaneously from within him. The rabbi who is a "mensch" normally judges people favorably and gives them the benefit of the doubt. Rabbi Feldman observes, "The rabbi must be generous even to a fault in judging and evaluating people, especially in his *voiced* judgments. No rabbi in his senses would speak ill of anyone in a eulogy; he must not do it to the living, either."

5. Be a lover of peace! Peace does not mean appeasement nor does it mean unprincipled compromise. The sage Hillel enjoined his colleagues to be "of the disciples of Aaron, loving peace and pursuing it." Peace must be a paramount value in a rabbi's life, and since it does not come easily, it must be pursued.

6. In a rabbi, a great capacity for friendship is vital. This does not imply descending to the lowest denominator of hilarity, or rolling up one's sleeves to become one of the boys. It does imply the capacity to trust and be trusted. Recently, a fascinating book was published by Carl Hermann Voss, entitled *Rabbi and Minister,* which depicts the friendship of Rabbi Stephen S. Wise and the great minister John Haynes Holmes. Their cooperative ventures in religious activity in New York transformed the moral face of that city. Wise, particularly, had a tremendous capacity for friendship. Stories were legion as to his phenomenal memory of the names and faces of even casual acquaintances. Because of his deep interest in people, Wise got to know them or at least something very important about them. Thereafter, whenever he met them, he could recall what it was that had tied him to these people. This was not a sham interest but a real concern for the people who entered into the orbit of Wise's life. Aristotle thought the capacity for friendship to be the single most important quality in human existence. In the rabbinate, it is a prized gift.

7. No rabbi has the right to be a snob. Within the rabbi's republic he must be a democrat. The rabbi may not succumb to what Rabbi Maurice Eisendrath has called, "the grievous failings of American culture—the worship of money, power, status, success—. . ." The rabbi must condition himself to show no overt favoritism to those who are well-heeled and to ignore those who are low at the heel. The rabbi's time and energy are available to all his congregants equally. As a religious leader, he ought not to favor powerful families in his congregation or important members of his community. Recently a colleague of mine related the story of a very important member of his congregation whose daughter had decided to be married on a certain date. The rabbi's calendar was already full for that day and he could not officiate at the ceremony without breaking a previous commitment. Some pressure was brought upon the rabbi to cancel his original date. The rabbi categorically refused. Contrary to what might have been expected, when he explained the ethics of the situation to the outraged "important member," the rabbi earned the respect and admiration of that man, as well as of the board of his congregation. The rabbi is more than a "profile in courage"; he must, indeed be the embodiment of courage.

8. A sense of humor is indispensable to the rabbinate. A profession which is highly charged with emotion, and propels the rabbi from one tension-laden situation to another, must be deflated. The rabbi may not take himself too seriously or he will become a paragon of pomposity and, ultimately, a source of derision to his people. After all, the rabbi is only human and capable of making mistakes, sometimes many of them; hopefully, not the same ones too often. Frequently a rabbi's sense of humor can take the winds out of the sails of animosity and create an atmosphere of relaxed amiability. I remember vividly one night when Dr. Stephen S. Wise was addressing a large audience in Brooklyn, New York. He was speaking against Nazism. Earlier that evening he had received a threat on his life if he were to go through with his address. Dr. Wise arose and, in his inimitable grand style, announced to the public: "I understand that an

attempt will be made on my life tonight. If the assassin is in the audience I beg him to shoot now; I should hate to be interrupted in the middle of my oration." The instantaneous response to Dr. Wise's profound sense of humor calmed the situation and, since the joke he told was on himself, he could well afford to enjoy his own laughter the most.

## SOME OF MY BEST FRIENDS ARE RABBIS, OR, SUCCESS IN THE RABBINATE

The rabbinate is a profession comprised of mortals. Although most rabbis seek to emulate scholars and saints, they are very *human* beings. With the exception of the ultra-orthodox rabbi who wears a distinctive garb reminiscent of medieval Europe, most men who are rabbis don't "look like rabbis." Although the good Lord has given to a handful of my colleagues the features of Michaelangelo's Moses, most rabbis look and dress like normal human beings. Without the tell-tale pulpit robe, on the face of it the rabbi is indistinguishable in a crowd. What differentiates him from others is his work.

There are very few rabbis who would admit to "receiving a call" from God or some divine power in the way this term is used in the Christian ministry. By contrast, Jews speak of "studying for the rabbinate." The aspiration to be a teacher of Judaism often serves as the motivating thrust to engage in rabbinic study.

A colleague of mine, Rabbi Edgar F. Magnin, with whom I have often discussed the question of what it takes to be a successful rabbi, has argued that the rabbinate is essentially an art. He makes the distinction between being arty and an artist; between affectation and basic drama; between a false stentorian voice and speaking with conviction. If the rabbinate is indeed an art, then we can only measure it by the artists who practice it. The consummate artistry of a Joshua Loth Liebman, a Milton Steinberg, a Rav Kook, is deserving of emulation. There is a considerable difference between emulation and imitation. A great rabbi used to admonish his younger imitators, "One of me is quite enough, perhaps too many. Be yourself!" He would also advise, "A voice of honey is no substitute for the salt of thought." The temptations to follow the patterns of "successful" rabbis is always present and represents the greatest pitfall for the young colleague. Whatever you have to give to the rabbinate is derived from your individuality, from the way you put together the great themes of Jewish history and play these through your person.

How shall we measure success in the rabbinate? It is clear from our tradition, as our sages said, "Take heed of the children of the poor, for from them will come forth the word of God." In the halls where Torah was studied, all men were equal. The rabbinate rewarded those who were part of the aristocracy of learning and who possessed the qualities of self-reliance and self-respect. Indicative of these qualities is a story recorded in our tradition of a certain rabbi who, having accepted an invitation to dine with the political leader of his day (Patriarch), responded, "I do not want to deprive His Excellency of the honor of my presence." This was not meant to be an arrogant statement but one which attempted to inform the Patriarch that it was an equal and not an underling whom he had invited. Arrogance among the aristocrats of learning was condemned. The sage Hillel said that whoever brags about his reputation will in the end lose it. Louis Ginzberg, in his classic volume, *Students, Scholars and Saints,* in discussing the authority of the *Talmid-hakham,* deduces that the rabbinic scholar drew his power

> . . . neither from the existence of a learned class nor in the constitution of the Jewish community. It was rather the personality of the scholar that gave him his prominent position. He was one whose mission was proclaimed by nothing in his apparel, but whose life and words made themselves felt in all hearts and consciences. He was of the people, and the people recognized themselves in him.

The times in which we live present some distorted images of success. Too often the second question that a rabbi is asked,

after he has introduced himself, is "How large is your congregation?" If the number is large, the assumption is that the rabbi
is the recipient also of a large salary, and his position is summed
up in the mind of the questioner as a "success." While there are
some rabbis in gray flannel robes who measure their own success
by the standards of a materialistic society, the vast majority of
men in the field weigh their achievements on other scales. Joseph
Zeitlin, in his depth study of the values of the American rabbinate, "Disciples of the Wise," came to the following findings
and conclusions:

> The preponderant majority of the American rabbinate is
> committed to a utilitarian moral philosophy.
>
> The rabbinate is well-nigh unanimous in its conviction that
> religion, to be a vital force, must identify itself with recon-
> structive social movements . . .
>
> A large proportion of the rabbinate see socially reconstruc-
> tive implications in the spirit of Judaism . . .
>
> The rabbinate in all its wings is preponderantly in favor
> of increasing social responsibility for the welfare and security
> of the individual . . .
>
> The rabbinate in all its wings is virtually unanimous in
> favoring the extension of the scope of social responsibility, for
> education beyond the prevailing level . . .
>
> Issues falling within the areas of philosophy of Jewish life,
> theology, and the social function of religion receive consider-
> able preaching emphasis . . .
>
> Moral principles constitute the ultimate basis of validity of
> any political, economic, and social arrangements . . .
>
> Democracy is the only pattern of social relations which con-
> stitutes a design for human living . . .
>
> Imperialism abroad and oppression and inequalities at

home which are based on racial differences are contradictory to the concepts of religion.

It is clear that the American rabbi measures his success or failure by the extent to which he has translated the ideology of Judaism into the life stream of society. The greater his artistry in imparting Judaism in all its ramifications, the greater is his success. He measures by the only standards which matter to him —the mandates of the "disciples of the wise."

Yes, some of my best friends are rabbis.

## CHAPTER III

## Studying for the Rabbinate

### PERSONAL QUALIFICATIONS

Preparing for the modern rabbinate usually means graduation from one of three major seminaries representing the three major branches of Judaism. The person who plans to make the rabbinate his career should begin serious exploration of his choice with one of the alumni of the seminary which he plans to attend. Normally, this would be his congregational rabbi, or the director of his Hillel Foundation, or some other rabbi active in the field of Jewish communal work. He will receive sound advice from his seasoned counselor, who will normally also put the prospective candidate in touch with the Director of Admissions of the seminary of his choice.

In addition to the desire to be a rabbi, the prospective rabbinic student must check his own personal qualifications to see whether, by interest and aptitude, he is capable of completing the seminary's training program. He should ask himself whether he has a consuming and abiding interest in Jewish affairs. Does he feel a very strong bond of affection for his fellow Jews everywhere? Is he anxious to lead and to help them? Is he convinced that Judaism, and his own specific religious way of life, can help modern Jews live more meaningfully? Is he anxious to prepare himself to interpret and teach Judaism in a manner that will make it come alive for the modern Jew?

Does he believe that there is a Power within human life and in the universe with which he and others can cooperate to strengthen themselves to build a better world? Does the candidate have an insatiable curiosity about things Jewish, and about the world in which he lives? Does he have the necessary human qualities, such as empathy, compassion, patience, tolerance for criticism, and general psychological stability? Does he recognize that the rabbinate is not an easy profession in which it is hardly likely that he will grow rich? While the rabbi may expect a decent standard of living and economic security, is the candidate prepared to place this in its proper relation to the other values which should animate him to enter the rabbinic field?

Toward the fulfillment of his ideals, is the candidate for rabbinic school prepared to work long and hard hours? Does he realize that his life is a public one and, very much like the physician, that he is virtually always on call? Is the person interested in the rabbinate aware that his family, like himself, will often be on public display? Is he willing to make the sacrifice of time and energy that will take him away from his family and his home a great deal of his waking and working time? If the prospective candidate for rabbinic study has been able to answer most of these questions in the affirmative, then he is ready to consider the requirements of the seminary of his choice, and is ready to receive the seminary's evaluation of him and his potential.

In addition to certain motivational factors relating to the candidate's personal qualifications, there are the additional considerations of physical and psychological fitness. Most of the seminaries require a physical examination of entering students which informs the school administration whether a candidate has a clean bill of health, or has some restriction on his physical activity. The Admissions Committee of the seminary must then determine, in light of the doctor's report, whether or not the candidate is capable of carrying out the long and taxing course of study without incurring undue physical strain and impairment to his health.

Students who pass the physical examination also undergo, in most seminaries, a psychological screening test. The purpose of this test is not merely to screen out emotionally unfit people, but also to give an indication to the school administration of the personal problems and limitations a candidate may have. Students of prerequisite intellectual ability and emotional stability usually clear this part of the admissions procedure without difficulty. The respective seminaries place varying degrees of emphasis on such tests. The Hebrew Union College–Jewish Institute of Religion and the Jewish Theological Seminary have increasingly placed a high degree of value upon them, considering them indicators of fitness for a rabbinic career.

With notable exceptions, the student has cleared up in his own mind where his theological preference lies by the time he applies for admission to one of the seminaries. A student's application is normally sponsored by an alumnus of the school, and this presupposes an acquaintance of the alumnus with the candidate for admission. Usually a recommendation for admission to one of the seminaries is not enough. Application forms are required to be submitted, giving some highly detailed personal information on one's background and education. Preparation for admission to the rabbinic schools varies considerably from seminary to seminary. The greater the candidate's background in Hebrew and in general Judaica, the more advanced is his standing upon admission. All of the three major seminaries, however, have made provision for the student who comes to them without any linguistic background, or with no more than a cursory acquaintance with the traditions of Judaism. For such candidates, special orientation programs are conducted, and normally their course of study is longer than that of the student who comes with adequate preparation.

EDUCATIONAL BACKGROUND AND APTITUDE

There are two questions which an undergraduate student who is a candidate for rabbinic study normally asks himself: What shall my major be in college; and how, as an undergraduate, may I better prepare myself for the seminary of my choice? As a condition for admission to the rabbinic department, which is a graduate school, the three major seminaries require completion of the baccalaureate degree.

The Jewish Theological Seminary and the Hebrew Union

College–Jewish Institute of Religion place a particularly high premium on a well-rounded liberal arts education. This requirement is predicated on the assumption that the modern rabbi must be able to relate his Jewish knowledge to general culture. Therefore, they require preparation in the fields of philosophy, history, psychology, language and literature, and the sciences. Since the rabbi must communicate well, careful attention should be paid to formal courses in English composition and literature. Both seminaries reserve the right, upon examination of a candidate's credentials, to require additional liberal arts courses should it be found that there are deficiencies in this area.

The usual admission procedure provides that, after all the required transcripts, recommendations and other documents are in the hands of the registrar, an oral interview be granted. This enables the faculty, who are members of the Admissions Committee, to become better acquainted with the student, and thereafter to advise him on a more personal and intimate basis. Normally, the catalogs of the seminaries provide the detailed information as to sequence of admissions procedures and special requirements. For example, the Hebrew Union College–Jewish Institute of Religion now requires that men entering the rabbinic department take the graduate record examination.

If you live in the metropolitan centers where the seminaries are located, it will usually be possible for you, as an undergraduate, to take courses in Hebrew language and literature and other subjects in Judaica. This will lead to better preparation for the ensuing more difficult studies, as well as advanced placement. If the candidate for admission to a rabbinic seminary lives outside such locales, study with an alumnus or with a tutor is recommended, after the candidate has received recommendations from the seminary as to specific requirements for admission. For example, the Hebrew Union College brochures state:

A knowledge of Hebrew, though highly desirable, is not a prerequisite for admission. If your Hebrew background is very elementary, we will ask you to begin your work with us in the summer preceding your first regular academic year, so as to enroll in our intensive course in biblical, rabbinic and modern Hebrew.

We are now ready to explore the specific requirements of admission, courses of study, scholarships and grants-in-aid, residence facilities, scholarly resources, and employment for the rabbinical student.

## VARIETIES OF JEWISH LEARNING

1. *Hebrew Union College–Jewish Institute of Religion (HUC-JIR) (Reform)*

*History and Programs*
The Hebrew Union College–Jewish Institute of Religion is America's oldest Jewish seminary with a continuous history. It was founded in 1875 by the architect of American Reform Judaism, Rabbi Isaac Mayer Wise. The Jewish Institute of Religion was established in New York by Rabbi Stephen S. Wise in 1922. Under the presidency of Rabbi Nelson Glueck, the two schools were merged in 1950. A third center of rabbinic training was developed in the fastest growing Jewish community in America, in 1954, when the Los Angeles school of the HUC-JIR was chartered. In 1963, a post-doctoral research center was opened in Jerusalem, known as the Hebrew Union College Biblical and Archeological School. Rabbi Glueck, a world-famed archeologist, has defined the character of the HUC-JIR schools as follows:

We are a liberal institution of higher learning in Judaism. Born and bred in the American scene, the College–Institute shares in the spirit of free inquiry and study which marks American colleges and universities. Unlimited academic freedom blends harmoniously with fidelity to Jewish institutions, as these have been shaped in Reform Judaism in the past 150 years . . .

The rabbinic schools in Cincinnati and New York offer the full rabbinic program. The California school presently offers only the first two years, leading to the Bachelor of Hebrew Letters degree; thereafter, the student transfers to Cincinnati. Undergraduate courses preparatory to the rabbinic program are available in Cincinnati and California. In Cincinnati, undergraduate work is taken at the University of Cincinnati and some course work, usually to the extent of six credits a semester, is taken at the HUC-JIR. The University of Cincinnati grants up to twenty-four credits toward the bachelor's degree for courses taken in the undergraduate program of the HUC-JIR. In Los Angeles, a similar arrangement exists with the University of Southern California, with whom the Los Angeles school has a specific affiliate relationship, as well as with the campuses of the University of California and the state universities. In New York City, the HUC-JIR provides a preparatory program through courses in its evening school. Since the HUC-JIR is an accredited institution, undergraduates may take course work in Hebrew language and literature, which then may be applicable to their liberal arts requirements at the university of their choice. Students enrolled in the preparatory and undergraduate programs pay tuition fees only to the university which they are attending. Scholarship aid is granted in the form of waived tuition at the schools of the HUC-JIR.

At the completion of the fourth year of the undergraduate program, the student takes the Hebrew readiness examination which tests his ability to handle elementary Hebrew texts and which, if successfully passed, admit him to the second year of rabbinic course work. The normal course of study at the schools of the HUC-JIR leading to ordination is five graduate years. A student commencing his pre-rabbinic course work while a freshman undergraduate, or a student who comes to the HUC-JIR with advanced standing, may make up one full rabbinic year or more through examination.

The first two years of graduate rabbinic study are terminated with a series of comprehensive examinations in classic Hebrew texts. After successful completion of this examination, the graduate student becomes a candidate in the rabbinic department. In his fifth year, or the last year of his rabbinic study, a candidate for ordination and the Master of Arts degree must present a scholarly thesis. While the Master of Arts degree is optional, most candidates for ordination take the comprehensive examinations required for the degree.

*Facilities*

The New York and Los Angeles campuses do not have dormitory facilities. In Cincinnati, beautiful dormitory, recreational, and dining facilities exist. The collective libraries of the four campuses represent one of the great collections in Judaica in the world. The Klau library in Cincinnati contains over 200,000 printed volumes and almost 6,000 manuscripts. The American Jewish Archives and the American Jewish Periodical Center constitute major research facilities in the field of American-Jewish history. The Jewish Museum, presently also housed in Cincinnati, is rich in its collection of Jewish art and artifacts. The New York school library contains 80,000 volumes and is especially strong in modern Hebrew literature. The Los Angeles campus has a well-rounded Judaica collection of 45,000 volumes. The College's Biblical and Archeological School in Jerusalem is primarily a postdoctoral research institution. A unique Reform service in Hebrew is conducted in its chapel.

*Tuitions, Scholarships, Bursary Aid*

The present tuition fee for graduate rabbinic students is $700 annually. The fee for residence at the Cincinnati dormitory is $1,000 for the academic year. In addition, a hygiene and health fee is required on all campuses, including medical and hospitalization plans. In all schools, bursary aid is available either in the form of deferred tuition, cash grants, or scholarships. No worthy student in need has ever been denied the opportunity of completing his rabbinic study due to insufficiency of funds while he was a student.

### Course of Study

The rabbinic school offers a vast array of courses from Akkadian, Arabic, Syriac, Ugaritic, and Greek to Hebrew language, Bible, Liturgy, Jewish Philosophy, Jewish Theology, Talmud and Commentaries, Midrash, and Homiletics. Extensive courses are provided in Jewish History, and in the general field of Hebrew Literature. Candidates for the rabbinate also take courses in Human Relations, Jewish Education, and Speech. A host of electives is available for upper-class students in addition to specialized preparation for writing their rabbinic theses.

### Field Training

During the student's years of study, many types of opportunity exist for earning a living. While these are necessarily of a part-time nature, they range from religious school teaching, youth group direction, or private tutoring to weekly and bi-weekly rabbinic assignments in the cluster of communities which surround the college campuses. Such employment opportunities are viewed by the college as training situations, and the student rabbinic positions are closely supervised by members of the faculty, who act as counselors.

If your interest is in the Reform rabbinate, then one of the schools of the Hebrew Union College–Jewish Institute of Religion is the place for you. Its viewpoint can be summarized in the words of its president, Dr. Nelson Glueck:

Nothing in the Jewish past or present is alien to our interest. We cherish the right of the free conscience to study Judaism, confident that the accurate and affirmatively critical and free study of our traditions will ensure its survival and enhance its sanctity.

2. *Jewish Theological Seminary of America (JTS) (Conservative)*

*History and Program*
The Jewish Theological Seminary of America is the Conservative movement's rabbinical training center, located in New York City. Chartered in 1886, it was the inspired instrument of Dr. Sabato Morais. Its present chancellor Dr. Louis Finkelstein is an oustanding talmudic scholar and brilliant administrator. The Seminary, which has as its motto "The preservation in America of the knowledge and practice of historical Judaism . . . ," was shaped to this image by Dr. Solomon Schechter. He became famous as the discoverer of the Cairo Genizah, in which cache thousands of ancient manuscripts were stored, which filled many lacunae in the knowledge of Jewish letters.

Dr. Schechter was committed to the ideal of "traditional yet scientific Jewish scholarship." He held that:

Judaism must stand or fall by that which distinguishes it from other religions as well as by that which it has in common with them . . . There is no other Jewish religion but that taught by the Torah and confirmed by history and tradition, and sunk into the conscience of catholic Israel . . .

This theological position, articulated by Dr. Schechter (1902-1915), still animates the Seminary today.

The Seminary's rabbinical department is described as "a graduate professional school training men for the rabbinate." The department encompasses the School of Judaica, which offers a one- to three-year course leading to the degree of Master of Hebrew Literature. The graduate rabbinical school accepts graduates of the School of Judaica, for whom it offers a three-year course leading to ordination. Rabbinic candidates who have completed their undergraduate education at accredited liberal arts colleges, and who are otherwise deemed qualified, must seek admission to the School of Judaica in order to complete the first phase of their rabbinic studies. The Seminary may require the maximum of three years in the School of Judaica for candidates who have insufficient background in Hebrew language and literature. Conversely, those who enter with considerable background may accelerate and complete their entire course requirement leading to ordination in four years.

The Seminary states as its requirement for admission to the rabbinical department that a student must be a member of the Jewish faith, conduct his life according to Jewish law and tradition, have high moral standards, and be observant of the Sabbath, festivals, daily prayers, and dietary laws. It has been the custom of the Seminary to require students to sign, as part of their application, a pledge that they will conduct themselves according to these principles.

The Seminary recommends the following courses as being helpful to students who are planning to enter the rabbinical department: English literature and composition; German or French; Latin or Greek; ancient, medieval, and modern history; philosophy, social sciences, and psychology.

Applicants are required to take a series of written and oral entrance examinations. These are divided into two parts. Part A consists of aptitude tests, preliminary interviews with members of the Admissions Committee, a qualifying examination, and, subsequent to that, interview with the entire Admissions Committee. Part B might well be considered a placement examination, which is also both written and oral. It encompasses knowledge of the Pentateuch with Rashi's commentary, and requires the candidate to translate sight passages from the Prophets, as well as to interpret selected passages. The Hebrew examination tests knowledge of Hebrew grammar and the ability to read and translate unpointed Hebrew texts, and requires the candidate to write a Hebrew composition and to converse in simple Hebrew. There is an oral examination in Talmud on a section that the student prepares, together with the commentary of Rashi. Lastly, there is a written examination which tests a general knowledge of Jewish history, as well as selected portions in the history of Jewish thought. The Seminary supplies bibliographies and other materials which will enable a student to adequately prepare for these examinations.

*Facilities*

The Seminary facilities for the training of rabbis provide a dormitory and an outstanding library of over 200,000 volumes and 10,000 manuscripts which, prior to the recent fire at the Seminary, was considered "the largest collection of Judaica ever assembled." The Seminary also sponsors an outstanding Jewish Museum with a valuable collection of Jewish ritual and art objects. Such cultural resources naturally buttress the academic program of the rabbinic school.

*Tutitions, Scholarships, Bursary Aid*

Tuition in the rabbinical department is $1,000 for the academic year, and the dormitory fee is $320. There is an additional fee for meals in the amount of $600. The Seminary provides tuition loans and scholarships to all students upon application. Students who require additional financial assistance may apply for short-term loans, and students who receive scholarships are expected to render some service to the Seminary during their first two years of residence.

*Course of Study*

The course of study of the School of Judaica concentrates on textual studies, Bible, Talmud, and Hebrew. The Seminary also conducts a preparatory department for the student who has received the baccalaureate degree and who is unable to pass part B of the examination due to insufficient background. This examination is then undertaken again at the end of his first year. Upon successful completion of the School of Judaica, the candidates who have earned the degree of Master of Hebrew Literature may apply to the graduate rabbinical school. Courses leading to ordination in the latter require three years of full-time residence study. Traditional Jewish studies in Bible, Hebrew, Talmud, Midrash, and Codes are continued, as are courses in Jewish history, philosophy and literature. The Seminary also requires specialized courses in professional areas, such as homiletics, education, practical theology, and pastoral psychology. Senior students may elect seminars which will help them gain knowledge in depth in selected areas.

*Field Training*

Field training is permitted for students in the rabbinical department in the form of part-time teaching positions and part-time rabbinic posts. Both the Hebrew Union College–Jewish Institute of Religion and the Jewish Theological Seminary have "internship" programs, in which cooperating rabbis aid in the training of a rabbinical student in the day-to-day work of the rabbinate. At the Seminary, this is reserved for members of the senior class. They are assigned to assist a rabbi, with whom they must conduct evaluation sessions of their work. The intern learns the rabbinic duties at worship services and ceremonies; he becomes familiar with the structure of the congregation and its school, its various auxiliaries and boards, the social welfare and other organizations in his community.

3. *Rabbi Isaac Elchanan Theological Seminary* (*RIETS*)
   (*Orthodox*)

*History and Program*

The Rabbi Isaac Elchanan Theological Seminary is described as "the leading school in the nation for the training of Orthodox rabbis." The school, which was the hub out of which Yeshiva University developed, evolved from two of the oldest *yeshivot* in the nation: Yeshiva Eitz Hayim, founded in 1886, and the Rabbi Isaac Elchanan Theological Seminary, founded ten years later for the specific purpose of providing intensive study in Talmud. The new Yeshiva was named in honor of Rabbi Isaac Elchanan Spektor of Kovno (1817-1896). He was one of the outstanding rabbinical figures of his generation and was famous for his Responsa, which were original in the new principles of legal interpretation which they espoused.

Yeshiva University, which today embraces several colleges and schools, has as its president Rabbi Samuel Belkin, a distinguished scholar in Jewish religious thought. Rabbi Belkin states:

> Yeshiva University takes great pride in its "uniqueness" as an institution of higher learning. This singular quality stems from its origins, which are rooted in two different systems of higher education. One is the *yeshiva,* a school of traditional learning where the Torah, Talmud, and other original sources of Hebraic culture are studied, and from which the university inherits its essential character as well as its spiritual, moral, and ethical core. The second is the *university,* after which it has patterned its complex of schools and divisions, each resting on deep-set foundation of liberal arts and sciences.

Rabbi Belkin further observes that, "traditionally and spiritually, the University is strengthened by those unique characteristics that it has inherited from the *yeshivot*—a sacred regard for knowledge and a devotion to the high moral and ethical values of Judaism." RIETS is modeled after traditional *yeshivot.* Torah is studied intensively with a great deal of emphasis placed upon the Talmud, Responsa literature, and the *Shulhan Arukh.* RIETS also trains rabbis who choose to be scholars, teachers, religious educators, and cantors.

### Facilities
RIETS is located in New York City, and offers housing to both undergraduate and graduate students. RIETS has an excellent library in Judaica and Hebraica, which is planned to be

incorporated in a projected new seven-story block-long central Yeshiva university library, designed to house its more than one million volumes.

### Tuitions, Scholarships, Bursary Aid

Tuition and fees are so structured that students who attend the Yeshiva College and RIETS simultaneously may do so with only a single tuition charge. Students in the *semikhah* program pay only a registration fee of $65. There is a *semikhah* fellowship program which aids gifted students, enabling them to devote full time to their rabbinic studies. Unmarried students may receive up to $1200 for the academic year, and married students, up to $2000. Unmarried students may receive an additional grant of $470 as a dormitory scholarship.

### Course of Study

At RIETS, *semikhah* represents "the oral or written conferral of rabbinical authority. It certifies that a man has qualified as a rabbi by virtue of intensive knowledge of the Talmud *halakhah* (codes) and his exemplary personal piety." He is presumed to be a master of both the oral and written traditions of Jewish law and lore.

The course of study at RIETS is divided into the college division and the *semikhah* program. Undergraduate students attend the University's liberal arts college and attend RIETS part time. The bulk of the college division courses at RIETS is in Talmud, with mastery of many of the major tractates. Courses also include biblical studies and training in Hebrew language, literature, and Jewish history.

Upon completion of the bachelor's degree a candidate may be admitted to the *semikhah* program, which takes three years of full-time study. Admission at RIETS calls for attendance at Yeshiva College, if the student does not hold a baccalaureate from another institution, and graduation from a Yeshiva University High School or a comparable school. The candidate must display a knowledge of Hebrew and intensive preparation (at least six years) in the Talmud. A knowledge of Bible and commentaries is also required. Admissions procedures call for individual oral examinations and placement examinations.

The graduate division *semikhah* program offers three major areas of concentration leading to the Master's degree: one is the Master of Science, obtainable in the Department of Religious Education of the Graduate School of Education; the Master of Arts in Semitics or Rabbinics, obtainable in the Bernard Revel Graduate School; and the Master of Hebrew Literature, obtainable from the same school. The last mentioned degree is geared to those intending to become pulpit rabbis. Professional courses in religious school administration, pastoral psychology, community relations, Jewish history, etc. are part of this program.

A student may substitute the *Kollel* program for the Master's programs. This provides "a special three-year course of intensified study in the Talmud and Codes," and is for students who are planning to make a career of teaching Talmud. Upon completion of the *Kollel* program of RIETS, the student must take comprehensive examinations which, when passed, yield the candidate the traditional *semikhah* and the title "rabbi."

## Field Training

The candidate for the Orthodox rabbinate also has much opportunity for field training. Teaching and rabbinic training positions are available for qualified students. No formal internship program is required, although informal supervision of students by graduates of RIETS is common.

## Other Jewish Seminaries

The Hebrew Union College–Jewish Institute of Religion is the only Reform seminary for the training of rabbis in America. The Jewish Theological Seminary represents the only training center in America for the rabbinate for the Conservative movement.

In addition to Yeshiva University's RIETS, there are a score of Orthodox *yeshivot*. Foremost among these is the Hebrew Theological College of Skokie, Illinois; Yeshivat Torah Vodaath

and Mesivta Rabbinical Seminary in Brooklyn, New York; the
Beth Midrash Gevoha, Lakewood, New Jersey; Central Yeshiva
Tomchei T'mimim Lubavich, Brooklyn; Rabbi Jacob Joseph
School and Mesivta, New York; Rabbinical College of Telshe,
Cleveland, Ohio; and Rabbi Hayyim Berlin Rabbinical Academy, Brooklyn. These Orthodox *yeshivot* represent particular
viewpoints within the spectrum of traditional Jewish thought,
ranging from the hasidic to the anti-hasidic. Most of these
*yeshivot* have their own alumni groupings and rabbinic associations. In these *yeshivot,* there are many students pursuing rabbinic courses who may or may not choose to be ordained. This
is true also of RIETS. It is not the case with the Hebrew Union
College–Jewish Institute of Religion and the Jewish Theological
Seminary of America. The students who enroll in these two seminaries seek to be ordained as rabbis and, upon graduation, wish
to practice their profession.

OPPORTUNITY FOR STUDY IN ISRAEL
    The three major seminaries, HUC-JIR, JTS, and RIETS, pro-
vide opportunities for overseas study for the seminarian. The
Hebrew Union College–Jewish Institute of Religion, in its Biblical and Archeological School in Jerusalem, offers supervised
study for students on leave from one of its American campuses.
Under the tutelage of the College's professors, students pursue
Hebrew, biblical and archeological studies related to the rabbinic
curriculum, combined with archeological field work. Students
may choose to reside in the dormitory facilities which are part
of the school. Encouragement is given by the institution, as well
as special scholarships and grants-in-aid, so that students may
take advantage of the opportunity for a year's study in Israel.
    The Jewish Theological Seminary of America maintains The
American Student Center in Jerusalem, which provides residen-
tial quarters for students of the rabbinical department on leave
for a year's study in Israel, for students of other Seminary
schools, as well as for alumni studying for advanced degrees.

The Seminary maintains a full-time resident faculty member who conducts seminars.

Yeshiva University maintains The Israel Institute, which is a part of the Bernard Revel Graduate School. One of the purposes of this Institute is to "develop an understanding and appreciation of the state of Israel and the problems which confront it in the face of *Halakhah,* Jewish history, and the culture and history of the Near and Middle East." To this end, courses are offered, and there is full reciprocity between the Bernard Revel Graduate School in New York and that in Jerusalem. Special emphasis is laid upon the study of legal problems, such as the nature of the rabbinic courts and their jurisdiction, as well as that of the Keneset. An attempt is made to analyze current legislation in the light of Jewish law. The institute also conducts public lectures and informal study sessions.

The three branches of American Judaism have established cultural centers in Israel for the purpose of creating a bridge between the two great centers of Jewish life. Each of the movements attempts to relate the significance of its philosophy to Israel, and that of Israel to its adherents in the diaspora.

NATIONAL AND INTERNATIONAL UNIONS OF JEWISH
CONGREGATIONS

Each of the seminaries serves a constituency of congregations which have combined into a voluntary association. The Union of American Hebrew Congregations (1873) represents at this writing 668 Reform congregations in the United States and Canada. The UAHC is the patron of the HUC-JIR. Regional offices of the UAHC are to be found in the major metropolitan centers of America. The Reform movement has a world-wide organization known as The World Union for Progressive Judaism, which has 114 congregations outside of the U.S.A. and Canada associated with it. The HUC-JIR student may elect to serve one of these World Union congregations during his years as a student rabbi.

The United Synagogue of America (1913) is the national as-

*Your Future as a Rabbi*

sociation of 785 Conservative congregations in the United States and Canada. It also maintains regional offices in major cities and has a number of commissions and departments associated with it to carry out the stated programs of the Conservative movement on a congregational basis. In 1957 the U.S.A. formed the World Council of Synagogues, which represents fifteen countries throughout the world. In 1959 a pre-rabbinic educational program was started for the regional office of the World Council of Synagogues in Buenos Aires, offering the preliminary courses leading to admission by the School of Judaica of the JTS.

The Union of Orthodox Jewish Congregations of America (1898) is the central body of Orthodox synagogues. One of its chief functions is to conduct a national *kashruth* certification service, in addition to carrying out the avowed program of the traditional community of America. The UOJC has not revealed the number of its member congregations since the definition of membership is somewhat hazy. At various times the UOJC has claimed to serve as many as 3100 congregations. A more realistic estimate would indicate that of the 1700 synagogues which call themselves Orthodox, only a portion could possibly be affiliated with the UOJC. The Orthodox community has no centrally organized world movement. There are, however, a number of sectarian Orthodox groupings which function on a world-wide scale. Among these are the Agudath Israel, which was founded in Europe in 1912 and organized in the United States in 1929; and the Hasidic Lubavitcher movement, followers of the Lubavitcher rabbi. There are other hasidic groupings which enjoy a world-wide following, although their collective numbers are not readily available.

RABBINICAL ORGANIZATIONS

When the seminarian has completed his course of study and is ordained, he is welcomed by the rabbinic fraternity of his particular movement. In the Reform movement this is the Central Conference of American Rabbis (1889). It has a membership of over 900 rabbis, most of whom were ordained at the Hebrew Union College–Jewish Institute of Religion or a comparable liberal seminary in Europe. The CCAR also has an alumni association which supports specific publications of the HUC-JIR and other worth-while projects. The CCAR meets annually, and through its resolutions, addresses itself to problems of world Jewry, war and peace, social and economic equality, and a host of other issues which relate to the interpretation of liberal Judaism on the American scene.

The Rabbinical Assembly (1901) is an international association of over 800 Conservative rabbis. It, too, convenes at annual assembly and seeks to implement the specific programs and ideologies of Conservative Judaism. The RA's constitution specifies that its purpose is:

. . . to . . . promote Conservative Judaism; to co-operate with the Jewish Theological Seminary of America and with United Synagogue of America; to advance the cause of Jewish learning; to promote the welfare of the members; and to foster the spirit of fellowship and co-operation among the rabbis and other Jewish scholars.

The Rabbinical Council of America (1923, reorganized 1935) is the largest and most influential association of Orthodox rabbis in the United States. Of its 830 members, about 600 are estimated to be in the active rabbinate, the rest being religious school administrators and teachers. The RCA meets annually and, like the CCAR and the RA, issues statements on the policy of the movement and on matters that are relevant to Jewish life. The members of the RCA are, for the most part, rabbis ordained at the Rabbi Isaac Elchanan Theological Seminary and the Hebrew Theological College of Skokie, Illinois. The remaining RCA membership is derived from graduates of other American and European *yeshivot*.

The various rabbinic associations have created a host of commissions to deal with the day-to-day work of developing their

respective movements. The Reform, Conservative, and Orthodox
rabbinic bodies publish the authorized prayer books, special
liturgies and religious tracts for their movements. They also publish *Year Books* containing the proceedings of their annual con-
ventions, as well as quarterly journals containing articles, sermons, and various other types of studies relating to the problems
of Jewish life in America and the world. From the three major
rabbinic organizations, chaplains are secured for the armed services. The associations also participate in or sponsor rabbinic
placement offices through which rabbis apply for new pulpits and
changes in pulpits. The various rabbinic organizations contain
on their rosters some of the greatest rabbis of America and the
world. They are formidable in advancing the interests of the
rabbinate in America.

## CHAPTER IV

## Ordained for Service

### SELECTING A FIELD OF SERVICE

The ordination ceremony, which marks the culmination of the rabbinic candidate's many years of study and training, propels him into Jewish life for full-time service to his people. His previous preparation through bi-weekly assignments, Hebrew teaching, a year abroad, or possibly an internship, all have aided the rabbi's growth and development. Often, the experiences of these formative student years shape a life's work in a given direction. A student may have found that he has considerable gifts as a preacher; another, that people are responsive in counseling situations; and still another, that he has enjoyed the varied contacts of active Jewish communal life. There are some who find themselves proficient as teachers and others who have a capacity for deep and ongoing scholarship. At ordination time, the rabbinic student, if he is free of chaplaincy obligation, begins to ask himself the fundamental questions as to the meaning of his impending rabbinate, and, depending upon how he answers these questions, seeks certain types of opportunities.

Graduating rabbinic students are normally placed by their seminaries. There are those already in the field, as well as those returning from chaplaincy duties, who also seek positions. They turn to the various rabbinic placement services, each of which has its own set of procedures and requirements. Within each movement, a fraternal code of ethics prevails, the breach of which jeopardizes the future placement of a rabbi.

The Yeshiva University's Community Service Division publishes the "Placement Procedures for *Musmachim*" (ordained rabbis). To qualify for placement, it is necessary to register with

91

the CSD, which involves a placement interview and clearance by the rabbinic alumni chaplaincy committee. Thereupon, registrants of the CSD are entitled to the benefits of the Yeshiva's placement procedures.

The Joint Commission on Rabbinic Placement, under the auspices of the Jewish Theological Seminary of America, the Rabbinic Assembly of America, and the United Synagogue of America, process Conservative rabbis seeking placement. The Joint Commission considers itself guided by the following considerations: (a) Requirements of the congregation, (b) Qualifications of the candidates, (c) Seniority of candidate, (d) Chaplaincy service, and (e) Needs of candidates.

The Rabbinical Placement Commission of the Reform movement is a joint commission also, representing the Central Conference of American Rabbis, the Union of American Hebrew Congregations, and the Hebrew Union College–Jewish Institute of Religion. This placement commission has published guidelines in rabbinic placement for both rabbis and congregations. It is the position of the Reform Commission that "a rabbi will not be considered for a change of position until he has been in his post long enough to have achieved some useful results." The Reform movement bases its placement on the size of the congregation, the length of service and experience of the rabbi, and additional guidelines for various situations and complexities that may arise. The Commission's placement procedures are absolutely binding on members of the Central Conference of American Rabbis.

Normally, placement procedure operates as follows: Due to either the retirement, resignation or dismissal of an incumbent rabbi, a placement commission declares a given pulpit to be vacant. It then officially informs the members of its affiliated rabbinic organization of the nature of the congregation and the categories of men who are eligible to apply for it. A panel of names is then drawn up. The names incorporated on the panel are derived from suggestions originating from within the congregation, recommendations by other rabbis, and the placement commission. The first panel, which may consist of one to six names, is then submitted to the congregation. The congregation chooses to interview one or as many of the rabbis as it feels qualify for its pulpit. The decision is then made by both the rabbis interviewed and the congregation to accept or reject the pulpit offer.

The interview procedures, while standardized by the rabbinic placement commissions, realistically vary with each congregation since the congregation is autonomous. Each congregation naturally attempts to find the rabbinic candidate best suited to its particular needs. Among the items that are discussed in the interview are the rabbi's theological views and their compatibility with those of the preponderant number of congregants; the scope of his responsibilities to the congregation and community; his salary, pension provisions, and emoluments or other benefits, such as housing, that the congregation may be willing to provide.

If the rabbi is interviewing for his first pulpit, either as an assistant or as the spiritual leader of a smaller congregation, the salary offered is probably in the vicinity of $8500 to $9000. If he seeks a Hillel Foundation directorship, the beginning salary is just over $9000. As part of his salary, the congregational rabbi receives a parsonage allowance which is legally deductible from his salary for income tax purposes. The sum of money is used to maintain his home.

As the rabbi grows in his profession and gains stature and recognition, he may choose to leave a situation where he has successfully met the challenge for yet more responsible and larger obligations. When he has reached this juncture, he again turns to the rabbinic placement commission of his particular movement and applies for congregations which offer him some advancement and the greater opportunity for service which he seeks.

CAREER OPPORTUNITIES

1. *The Military Chaplaincy*
Service to men in the armed forces is an important factor in rabbinic placement. The major seminaries require that all men

who are physically and psychologically fit, who have not had previous military service and are not conscientious objectors to war, volunteer to serve in the military chaplaincy if they are needed. Since clergymen, by law, cannot be drafted, it has required the inner discipline of the three branches of American Judaism to assure the armed forces that a sufficient number of Jewish chaplains is available to minister to the needs of Jewish military personnel. World War II, particularly, made of the chaplaincy a moral and patriotic commitment on the part of the rabbinate. Rabbi Bertram Korn, commemorating the centennial of the Jewish chaplaincy of the United States, has written of the fascinating Reverend Jacob Frankel, cantor of Rodef Sholom Congregation of Philadelphia, who in 1862 "achieved the distinction of becoming the first Jewish chaplain to be commissioned by the American government, or by any government for that matter, for ministration to Jews in the uniform of their country."

Since World War I, the National Jewish Welfare Board has been recognized by the American government as the agency which provides "religious and moral services to the Jewish military personnel and veteran hospital patients." JWB recruits, endorses, helps to train, and supervises Jewish chaplains for the armed services. It furnishes them with religious supplies, literature, and program aids. When World War II broke out, a committee on army, navy, and religious activities of JWB was organized, which was composed of representatives of the three religious groups within the American rabbinate. This committee, which now bears the name of the Commission on Jewish Chaplaincy, is completely under the control of the three major rabbinical organizations of the country. Its policies are determined by the rabbis themselves, and its leaders are men who have served as chaplains.

As standing armies continue to be part of the military preparedness program of our country, the need for chaplains will remain. During World War II it was estimated that about half the eligible rabbis of the United States offered themselves for chaplaincy service. Of those who applied, 422 received endorsement and 311 actually served. Most chaplains volunteer for a period of two to three years, but there are some rabbis who choose the military chaplaincy as a permanent career. Recently the Commission on Jewish Chaplaincy formulated a plan which was approved by JWB's executive committee, aimed at converting the Jewish chaplaincy from a corps of men, most of whom serve a limited tour of duty through a voluntary draft system, to a group of largely career chaplains who would serve twenty years or more. Seventy Jewish chaplains are needed, forty of whom it is hoped would be career chaplains, and thirty who would be short-term chaplains. Upon completion of twenty years of military service, the chaplain receives a life pension of from $5000 to $6000. New men will be required to fill posts upon the retirement of an increasing number of Jewish chaplains who made the chaplaincy their career after World War II.

During World War II, Jewish chaplains played a heroic role in aiding the victims of Nazi oppression. These chaplains worked miraculous acts of deliverance in helping to set up the necessary social agencies for the survivors of the concentration camps. They performed many acts of mercy and assisted survivors who wished to leave Europe to go to Israel and other lands. Perhaps the dedication of the chaplaincy may best be illustrated by the bravery of the four chaplains, one of whom was Rabbi Alexander D. Goode. The four chaplains were on duty on the transport *Dorchester* in the north Atlantic when the ship was struck by a torpedo. The chaplains gave their life belts to members of the ship's crew, as there was a shortage, giving up their own lives for others. As the vessel was sinking, a last view of the chaplains found them standing at the ship's rail deeply engrossed in prayer.

The list of rabbis on the roster of organizations working for peace throughout the world is as long as the rabbis' voices have been vigorous. Yet when war occurs, they have responded to help those who are embroiled at the front lines of conflict. Chap-

lain Edward T. Sandrow wrote from Alaska during World
War II:

> Never in my life have I seen men so eager for spiritual ex-
> pression as I have found them here. . . . Restlessness and
> intense activity do not deter them from religious fellowship.
> . . . Wherever I have gone, hungry men have literally lapped
> whatever drops of spiritual nourishment I could give them.
> Religion is a matter of tremendous concern to these men. The
> power of faith—our faith—is the answer. I can better under-
> stand our history now. Backgrounds dissolve; the same thirst
> and yearning for God remains.

The Jewish chaplain represents the value system of Judaism
to the serviceman. He is the serviceman's confidant, friend and,
most important, the link to his home and his family. By virtue
of his role, the Jewish chaplain has been an interpreter of
Judaism to large numbers of non-Jews. A chaplain must also
be ready to minister to the needs of men of other faiths. As part
of his daily work, the chaplain conducts services and ceremonies,
cares for the sick and wounded, buries the dead, teaches and
counsels the soldier on his problems.

The chaplain, too, has problems as he struggles with his own
conscience when assisting the forces that engage in war. Rabbi
Harry Nelson summarizes the chaplaincy situation as follows:

> We have many problems confronting us. We are in the
> midst of a bitter struggle between East and West. Men are
> still being called upon to serve in our armed forces. We must
> provide chaplains for them. We hope that they will serve in
> peace and that they will never again be called to lead men
> in war.

2. *The Pulpit Rabbi*

By far the largest number of rabbis who are active in their
field occupy pulpits. The pulpit rabbinate is one of the most

challenging, rewarding and complex of callings. The rabbi is elected by his congregation or its board to serve them. Rabbi Emanuel Rose recently observed that the rabbi's

> . . . rights and obligations do not derive from the congrega-
> tion . . . A rabbi must feel his strength and security not in
> the numbers (although they are very comforting to be sure)
> who agree, but in his deep belief in and commitment to the
> ethical validity of his position.

The rabbi voices with conviction the sense of values that he con-
ceives to be his mandate in the teaching of Judaism to his people.
A strong rabbi directs the religious affairs of his congregation
with vision and courage and is prepared for frustration and
opposition. For, if all Jews were prophets, there would hardly
be a need for him or his vocation.

Because Jewish congregations are highly individualistic and
since Judaism lacks a religious hierarchy, the rabbi's success depends upon his talents as persuader. The story is told of a rabbi
and a priest discussing their respective difficulties. The priest said
to the rabbi, "I can't tell you how difficult it is to be a priest of
a parish of 500 Catholic communicants," to which the rabbi
replied, "And you can't imagine how difficult it is to be the rabbi
of a congregation of 500 rabbis." The rough-and-tumble of the
democratic process is nowhere as evident as in congregational
life. It is no longer possible even for the Orthodox rabbi to take
refuge in tradition alone; he, too, is often subject to the challenge and consensus of his congregation. The modern rabbi must
remain relevant and talk in the language of his people.

The congregational rabbi's work is mostly with his congregants. Normally, he supervises the religious school, and may or
may not be the actual principal of that school. He teaches the
confirmation class; develops and participates in adult education
programs; directs the religious affairs of the auxilliary groups of
his temple, men's and women's clubs, youth groups, and allied
boards. Foremost among his obligations is that of religious

leader in public worship, fearlessly preaching the mandates of
Judaism, ministering to the sick and the bereaved, and counseling those who are troubled. There are many more community
obligations which have already been delineated. The congregational rabbi must be sincere, a man of great energy and vision,
who can meaningfully conduct the affairs of his congregation.

At the Central Conference of American Rabbis' Convention
in 1963, a rare symposium took place between Rabbi Solomon
B. Freehof of Pittsburgh and Rabbi Abba Hillel Silver of Cleveland. Both men had made exceptional careers in the pulpit. In
the symposium, the rabbis asked one another about the standards
of success and failure in their rabbinates. In response to Rabbi
Freehof's question, "What should be the prime function of a
rabbi?" Dr. Silver replied,

> I know that many other duties are demanded of the modern
> rabbi, many of which he must perform—pastor to his flock,
> tribune of his people to the non-Jewish world, defender of
> social justice and the rights of man. But principally, in my
> humble judgment, the rabbi, as the name signifies, is teacher
> —not pastor, but teacher. By teaching young and old the
> spiritual and ethical documents of Judaism, and thereby in-
> spiring in them a life of personal integrity and social responsi-
> bility, the rabbi makes his major contribution to his individual
> communicants, to his congregation and to his community.
>
> I know that is not a sensational answer; that's the answer
> I can give you.

Rabbi Silver then asked Rabbi Freehof about success in the
rabbinate, to which the rabbi replied, "I would count the rabbi's
success by how many people he trains to divine worship. Now,
this may be an outward sign, but it also may be what the Episco-
palians call the 'outer visible sign of an inner visible quest.'"
Rabbi Silver was asked what was the greatest obstacle in a
rabbi's career, to which he replied,

The rabbi himself. I mean, his inherent deficiencies. If a rabbi lacks character or courage or tact or sensitivity, he is likely to destroy his own career.

If he sets his heart on false objectives, in quest of excessive publicity—we all like a certain amount of publicity—or on being well-liked by everybody, or on never saying anything that will not be approved by everybody, that rabbi will corrode himself from within, in the long run.

Rabbi Silver also pointed to other obstacles that rabbis encounter: the inertia of people, the sluggishness of progress, and downright opposition. But "these will not destroy or even retard his true career. They will temper, strengthen him, and help him to fulfill his career." No better advice could be given to the young man who aspires to prominence in the pulpit. Certainly, obstacles and frustrations are inevitable in the rabbinate but so are its great and irreplaceable moments of triumph and achievement.

### 3. *The Assistant and Associate Rabbi*

In larger congregations the rabbi will often require an assistant. The assistant is usually a recent graduate of his seminary who has placed himself under the tutelage of a more experienced rabbi. Normally, the assistant will have specific charge of the educational program of the synagogue or temple, and will assist the rabbi in his many duties. The assistant is not an errand boy but a colleague who has apprenticed himself so that he may learn his rabbinic craft from a seasoned man. A graduate will gravitate toward a senior rabbi whose career he wishes to emulate and from whom he believes that he can learn a great deal.

An assistantship may sometimes grow into an associateship, in which case rabbinic duties are shared equally. In larger congregations where there is more than one assistant, certain aspects of the work may be distributed so that the senior rabbi preaches, and the educational and pastoral work is assigned to the assistants. There is much variation within each congregation, depending upon the inclinations and talents of its rabbis. An assistant-ship lasts, on the average, for a period of two to three years. The young rabbi then usually assumes responsibility for a congregation of his own.

### 4. *The Rabbi as College Professor*

Recently at a press conference, Dr. Glueck predicted that within the next decade, fifty chairs of Judaica would be developed on the major campuses of the United States. There has been a growing trend to establish chairs of Hebrew language and literature, and chairs of Judaica at large metropolitan campuses where a sizeable number of Jewish students is enrolled. The seminaries which have grown within this last decade also require additional teachers. There have always been rabbis who were college professors, not a few of whom became distinguished scholars.

There are scores of other rabbis who engage in part-time teaching at seminaries, Jewish and Christian, and at various universities throughout the land. The directors of Hillel Foundations, in particular, find themselves called upon to teach courses in Bible or Jewish Religious Thought on the campuses at which they serve. The new turn of events at universities, however, is to look for full-time professors of Judaica, who would make college teaching their life's work. Usually, the universities turn to the rabbis to fill these vacancies. An ever-growing number of rabbis have earned their doctorate degrees either in Hebrew letters or philosophy and thereby hold the proper credentials for appointment to professorial posts. This is an exciting new development on the American-Jewish scene and provides an excellent opportunity for men who want to train themselves for this particular vocation and devote their entire energies to teaching and research.

### 5. *The Rabbi as Hillel Director*

The Hillel Foundation has long offered a unique opportunity for the rabbi interested in teaching and counseling college-age youth. Hillel work is immensely gratifying to rabbis who thrive in an intellectual atmosphere. Dr. Alfred Jospe has written that "For nearly four decades, B'nai B'rith Hillel Foundations have functioned as the bearer and symbol of Jewish life in the university community." During these years, Hillel has grown from one foundation serving a few hundred students at the University of Illinois into a network spanning the North American continent, Europe, Israel, Australia, and South Africa. Two hundred and fifty-seven Hillel Foundations (a Foundation is a full-time operation with a full-time Director in charge, and usually with a building of its own) are located in the United States and Canada and serve a quarter of a million Jewish students. Twenty Hillel Foundations are located overseas; the remaining Hillel units are Counselorships involving part-time supervision by a neighboring congregational rabbi, Jewish educator or faculty member.

The Hillel Foundations maintain three chairs of Judaic studies: the Hillel professorship of Jewish Thought and Literature at Vanderbilt University, the Hillel professorship of Jewish Studies at the State University of Iowa, and the Hillel professorship of Hebrew Studies at the School of Religion of the University of Missouri. In addition, there are a number of regional directors who supervise given geographic areas.

It is the task of the Hillel director to serve all the Jewish students on his campus and to provide for such individual religious services as the student constituency of his Foundation might request. The Hillel director is "a link between the Jewish college student and his heritage." The functions of the Foundations have been defined by students themselves as ranging from "the place where I can work out a sound basis for a personal philosophy of Judaism" to "a place for Jewish kids to meet." Dr. Jospe observes:

Specifically, the Hillel program encompasses activities which seek to provide the Jewish student, through study and discussion, with adequate and accurate knowledge of Jewish life by acquainting him with the faith, the literature, the history and life and thought patterns of the Jewish people; which enable him to share in the religious and cultural Jewish expressions of the Jewish heritage with understanding and appreciation; and which will provide him with the opportunity to express his personality in activities aiming at the perpetuation and development of the Jewish religio-cultural heritage.

The Hillel rabbi participates in the education of the Jewish college student in his most formative years, and often the imprint that he is able to leave upon his charges shapes their view of Judaism in their more mature years.

The Hillel directors have their own organization and discipline. Salary scales range from over $9,000 to $15,750 for full-time directors, depending upon years of service and the extent of the director's responsibility. Assistant or associate directors receive somewhat less than the minimum scale. The professional staff of the B'nai B'rith Hillel Foundations is covered by a full insurance program, which is funded by the organization and the participant. The over-all coverage includes retirement insurance, life insurance, major medical plan, and other benefits.

## 6. *The Non-Military Chaplaincy*

A number of rabbis serve as chaplains in various types of institutions, such as hospitals, mental institutions, prisons, homes for the aged, and orphanages. The work of the community chaplain may, at times, encompass most of these. In large metropolitan centers, the Jewish Federation Councils, in conjunction with a host of auxilliary agencies, provide a chaplain whose task it is to bring religious programming and pastoral counseling to a wide variety of people in need. In addition to conducting services, such chaplains engage in counseling activities, ranging from helping to find work for a parolee to making a family cognizant of its responsibilities to one of their members who is institutionalized. The non-military chaplain is virtually a social worker who, because of his talents as religious counselor and Jewish resource person, is engaged in a plethora of activities to bring help and comfort to people. While many rabbis, particularly those in smaller communities, perform these functions as part of their regular congregational work, the full-time non-military chaplaincy has definitely developed into a highly specialized field.

Rabbi Samuel W. Chomsky has made himself expert as a Jewish chaplain in matters pertaining to veterans. Rabbi Chomsky points out that the Veterans Administration chaplain is primarily a hospital chaplain who works mostly with the acutely ill. He finds that counseling chronic and geriatric patients requires special skills to offset the fears and terrible loneliness of such victims. The VA chaplain also deals with mental patients, both young and old. Very often these people need ongoing encouragement in order to help them resume a normal life. In order to assist such patients, the chaplain uses different kinds of counseling skills, including religious services. It is vital to impart to these patients the feeling that someone cares deeply about them. Rabbi Chomsky observes, "An impersonal ministry would sometimes do more harm than no ministry at all." The chaplain, who represents the religious values of the Jewish tradition to these patients, has found that prayer is a deeply felt need by patients, since it relates to the concepts of faith, courage, hope, security, peace, and strength. Through prayer they feel the presence of God in their lives, and often this gives them the impetus to help themselves and to restore health of mind and of body.

The Jewish chaplain in mental hospitals is becoming very important. Dr. Abraham N. Franzblau, in an address entitled "Functions of a Chaplain in a Mental Hospital," raises the question as to whether it is the function of the chaplain to administer therapy. Therapy can be viewed in either broad or strict terms. If one were to regard it as a skilled technique to be administered only by rigorously trained professionals, then many chaplains would be excluded from therapy situations. However, therapy is a very difficult term to so confine. All of its definitions imply helping to find a cure. While some patients have mental illnesses that do not yet respond to known cures, there are nevertheless ways in which these people can be made more comfortable. Rabbis and candidates for rabbinic training who devote time to patients in mental hospitals often find themselves involved in therapy conferences. They report of patients who yearn for someone to talk to, someone who would respond to them. The mere proximity of another human being not institutionalized, who did not *have* to care, restored sparks of hope in some patients who had well-nigh concluded that the world outside was not one whit affected whether they lived or died, whether they recovered or rotted away. Dr. Franzblau observed that the rabbi can do something which is very important and unique in the life of a patient. He can often assist in restoring the judgment of an individual and help him recover his sense of objectivity.

Unquestionably, rabbis who specialize as chaplains for work in mental institutions must take training in psychology, not only to understand their patients but also to understand themselves. However, if a rabbi is called upon to do extensive psychiatric counseling, there is no substitute for intensive graduate work, qualifying him as a clinical psychologist. He may even go the full way, studying medicine and becoming accredited as a psychiatrist. In the profession of chaplain there is no room for amateurs. This is serious work involving the sanity and life of other human beings. The chaplain's training cannot be improvised or extemporaneous. Nothing will take the place of systematic study and certification.

The chaplain who deals primarily with the emotionally and mentally disturbed must also have certain personal qualities. Rabbi Jerome Folkman observes, "Empathy is the basis of every counseling situation. The counselor must earn the right to counsel. He must earn it anew in each case." Unquestionably, it will take a special kind of human being to make a success of this highly complex career of ministering to the mentally ill.

The role of the correctional chaplain requires yet a different kind of specialization. Rabbi Isser L. Freund points out that the office of the correctional chaplain was originally not set up by the penal institutions themselves. In most cases ministers and representatives of religious organizations concerned with "the forgotten men in the jails . . . worked themselves into the correctional system and brought solace, hope and, sometimes, a little extra food to the imprisoned." Gradually, the correctional chaplaincy became a profession in which the chaplain performed more than his priestly duties in prison confines. Rabbi Freund points out that "his functions and personality permeate the whole life of the prisoner and the prison community." While the chaplain preaches and teaches the principles of his faith, he does more.

He is the father-image to the rejected; he is the listener without a report; he is the conscience without chastisement; he is the sounding board for hostilities without disciplinary action; he is the eternal optimist where despondency reigns; he walks around without a club and power; he looks at pictures of wives and children left behind; he is tolerant of sins without peeking into subterranean personality gutters; he rationalizes authority rather than enforces it; he listens (if he is wise, and most of them are) without interpretation; he is gullible without reprisal; he is soft in an environment where everything else is harsh; he is sympathetic even when one does not deserve it; he is a symbol of the family from which the prisoner is severed, and of the community from which he was separated or expelled; he is the liaison with the world outside, from which the prisoner is excluded and to which he passionately hopes to go back. He is high-minded and humble; he is re-assuring that no life is worthless or completely depraved in the sight of God.

In this moving statement, Rabbi Freund has brilliantly summarized the universal role of the rabbi, not just the chaplain in the correctional institution. There are not a great number of rabbis who seek this kind of hard and challenging work as their vocation. Yet, to serve the disinherited and the unwanted repre-

sents one of the highest callings within the Jewish faith. It is
hoped that more competent rabbis can be secured for this immensely interesting and inner rewarding field of the non-military
chaplaincy.

### 7. *The Rabbi as Executive Director*

In addition to the already described career opportunities,
there is one we may label "the rabbi as executive director." This
catch-all description covers those men who are essentially administrators. The national Jewish organizations, such as congregational unions, B'nai B'rith, the American Jewish Committee, Zionist organizations, and a host of others, may engage
rabbis, both on a national and regional level, as program con-
sultants or as executives. Such work normally takes the rabbi out
of congregational activity and propels him into organizational
work, writing and editing journals and newspapers, fund-raising,
organizing membership drives, public relations, and many other
allied activities. One might very well ask why it was necessary to
be an ordained rabbi in order to do such work. The institutions
engaging rabbis for these purposes would readily reply that the
knowledge of Jewish tradition and history that the rabbi brings
to the organization, as well as his normally superior intellectual
qualities, are very valuable to them. The rabbi is a vital resource
person who may have much influence in shaping the content and
form of Jewish organizational life.

While not an appreciable number of rabbis are engaged in
this type of work, all indications are that this category of employment is growing. As Jewish institutional life becomes more
complex, more rabbis will become interested in affiliating with
national and regional organizations. The gratification in this
kind of work for the rabbi comes from a clearly defined area of
responsibility in a stable organizational structure, and the opportunity of affecting large numbers of Jews. It may provide him
with the chance to write and speak extensively; in short, allow-
ing a greater platform for his ideas. Because most organizations
have the resources, he may also undertake research projects and

depth studies on the many significant problems relating to the survival of Jewish life. While most rabbis will not give up the satisfactions of the congregational rabbinate, there will be some who will see in the executive directorship new opportunities to be of service to their people and who will feel themselves challenged to undertake them.

### 8. *Ancillary Professional Training for the Rabbi*

In order for the rabbi to function effectively, he must garner skills which may not have been taught in depth in the highly specialized seminary program. Among these are pastoral counseling, social work and community relations. The congregational rabbi often is called upon to function in such areas and should show proficiency in them.

Some of the seminaries offer introductory courses in human relations, in which basic information of normal and abnormal psychology is imparted. The rabbinic student is made aware of the ebb and flow in the human life cycle. He is expected to become conscious of his own limitations and problems, since he must guard against projecting these upon those who seek his counsel. Such courses deal with the principles of group dynamics and social action. The role of the rabbi is critically examined as is the structure and value system of the contemporary synagogue. Community problems are investigated and the functions of social agencies are analyzed.

The rabbinic candidate is somewhat prepared to face the counseling or pastoral role, but he is far from expert in it. In all these relationships and roles, neither rabbinic student nor ordained rabbi must ever lose sight of the fact that Jews are turning to him for guidance because he is a rabbi. His counsel should bear the impress of Jewish values while adhering to accepted guidance procedures. Rabbi Robert L. Katz, a specialist in "Human Relations," has observed that because modern rabbis "will engage in more face-to-face counseling of individuals," they will "cease to rely exclusively on intuitive methods of counseling and will avail themselves of some of the insights, techniques, and cautions that have already been defined in the field of pastoral psychology." This means that the rabbi's education in this area of his work must be on-going.

The normal areas of rabbinic counseling deal with the problems of marriage, divorce, educational and vocational difficulties and adjustments, illness, bereavement, and crises of various other kinds. The rabbi constantly deals with the question of religious faith or the loss thereof, as well as with the individual on the verge of conversion into or out of the Jewish faith. There are also a host of other problems brought to the rabbi—some not worthy of his time, others so complex that he should not become involved at all. The story is told of the Jewish matron who insisted upon seeing her rabbi because she suffered from a terrible headache. After telling her story in a torrent of words and screams, she finally paused to catch her breath and observed that her headache was gone. The rabbi moanfully replied that he was glad she had lost *her* headache, but as far as he was concerned, she had merely transferred it to *him*.

Even the rabbi who does not consider pastoral counseling his forte is obliged to acquaint himself with the rudiments of therapy, if only to protect himself from making harmful mistakes which may adversely affect the lives of others. Because the role of the clergyman is growing and his authority as a spokesman for religion in the lives of families is recognized, he will be sought out with increasing frequency to counsel. A good heart and thoughtfulness are vital to successful counseling but there are other traits that must be acquired if the rabbi is to be effective. Rabbi Katz wisely admonishes, "When the rabbinical counselor listens, he should not pride himself on the open but untrained ear." An overzealous counselor can do as much harm as no counselor at all. He must know where to draw the line. When the rabbi is presented with complex problems involving a great deal of time, he would be prudent to refer the people to the proper agencies with the appropriate professional personnel. If the rabbi is wise, he will make a study of all the community resources available to which he might direct people whenever possible and desirable.

In the early days of the American rabbinate, when congregations had special committees whose responsibility it was to take care of the indigent, people in search of work and people in trouble, the synagogue served as a treatment center, however temporary such treatment may have been. A number of congregations, particularly the Free Synagogue in New York, created a special Department of Social Service, which handled child adoption, care for the aged and the troubled.

Today the picture is quite different; ordinarily, rabbis who are in close contact with the social service agencies and their staffs work with them on such matters. There is hardly a community in America today, in which there is a sizeable concentration of Jews, that does not have a Jewish Family Service. Very often the rabbi is the key person, either as negotiator or as sponsor, from whom a reference is sought. His reputation for keeping confidences must be impeccable, and his usefulness as a lay social worker is often measured by the extent to which he can help a person quietly and efficiently. If the rabbi has a charitable fund, he will undoubtedly make proper use of it to help people in crisis situations whose problems might be solved by immediate assistance. Where such funds are lacking, there is always the Hebrew Free Loan Society to which the rabbi can turn, as well as generous members of his own congregation.

Rabbi Sidney Goldstein who, for many years, thrust the activities of the Free Synagogue into the social arena, has wisely taught:

The social ideals born of the souls of the Prophets can be realized only as they are painfully and courageously worked into the fabric of our social life. This the Rabbi cannot accomplish alone. He must labor with and through men and women and groups and institutions. While the Rabbi is not a professional social worker he is interested in the objectives of social work and must seek to participate in it on his own level of competency, experience and interest.

As teacher of the young, the rabbi is involved in youth work and camping. This area is developing as a distinct profession for a number of rabbis. There are some men who are more talented than others in working with youth; others have grown up with the various youth movements and show aptitude and preference for this type of work. They prepare themselves to become the professional heads of the youth and camping divisions of their respective movements. The national religious groupings have extensive programs for youth which supplement the formal study of the religious school. Often the camp and the youth programs are seen as extensions of the religious school. Supplementary curricula are prepared to make maximum use of these activities, which may take place outside the confines of the synagogue structure.

Every rabbi, however, is called upon at some time or another to involve himself in these types of programs and he must take great pains to prepare himself when such opportunities arise. A particular sensitivity is required to be successful in this work, and the rabbi needs to know in detail the problems that confront youth. Last summer, when I was involved in a leadership training seminar in one of the Reform movement camps for "Living Judaism," the subject that was scheduled to be taught was "The Hebrew Prophets." It became very clear, however, from the first moment of encounter with the young people who were nearing draft age, that their immediate concern was the issue of war and peace: their personal involvement in the military and the reconciliation of that involvement with the values that Judaism teaches. It took a skillful staff of rabbis to adapt the prepared materials to the particular needs of that encampment.

The rabbi is a communal leader. While he cannot participate actively in all the causes in which he is interested (for he could spend his entire day attending worth-while meetings), he must nevertheless choose some with which he will have maximum involvement. The congregation which he serves is part of a larger community, and both the rabbi and his congregants need to involve themselves in the welfare of that community. It is unwise for the rabbi to assume roles other than that of spiritual leader, energizer, spokesman, and teacher. In matters of community interest, the rabbi must be careful to attack issues and not personalities, to stand above the political manipulations that inevitably trouble every organization, and stick to the religious and moral issues involved. The rabbi should strive to stand above the crowd and be a battler for principles rather than petty interests.

A new word has found coinage recently in the religious vocabulary of Americans. It is "ecumenicity." This term, which had a rather limited meaning prior to the far-reaching conclusions of the second Vatican Council, connoted a sort of worldwide reciprocity of recognition among Christian denominations. It has now been stretched to include non-Christian religions as well. Ecumenicity goes beyond tolerating other religions to seeing inherent worth in them. While there had been considerable interfaith activity prior to the deliberations of the Vatican II, the October, 1965, declaration on the relation of the Catholic church to non-Christian religions opened the portals of the church for searching dialogue with other religions. A large body of the world's populace, which is Catholic, will now be able to officially relate to Jews as well as to other non-Catholic Christian communions because the Council's declaration has swept away, in important measure, ancient grievances and hates which have no place in the modern world. A massive breakdown in stereotyped thinking is taking place as Christians and Jews begin to face one another to discuss their common traditions and destinies.

The condemnation of anti-Semitism by the First Assembly of the World Council of Churches (Protestant), in 1948, and now the Catholic schema on the Jews which "decries hatred, persecutions, displays of anti-Semitism," will chart new ways in interfaith programming. Increasingly, the rabbi will be called upon, as he has already experienced, to engage in interfaith dialogue and seminars. It has been customary for some time and in some communities for rabbis and ministers to exchange pulpits in order to explain their respective faiths; however, programming in depth is now under way so that a full meeting can take place between Christians and Jews. The rabbi's training and attitudes will need to become schooled to this new phase of clerical activity, and he will have to prepare himself to discuss the beliefs and principles of Judaism on the most profound and scholarly levels with men of comparable training and experience in the Christian ministry.

So much depends on attitude in interfaith work. Past rebuffs and animosities must be forgotten, and new attempts made to reach understanding and appreciation for what has been called the Judeo-Christian heritage. The rabbi will find it necessary to begin to train his fellow Jews also, and prepare them for an ecumenicity which will provide equal representation for the Jewish layman in the religious affairs of the modern world. Joint commissions of Jews and Christians on civil rights, war and peace, poverty and education, have already begun to develop. The rabbi will need to stretch his knowledge to include an historical understanding of the development of Christianity and its many denominations. In any event, this newest phase of rabbinic activity will propel the rabbi into yet other facets of inter-religious community life.

The Jewish people want and expect the teachers of their faith to be involved in vital areas of community activity and demand their participation in decisions that affect the community. Not a charitable campaign is waged, not a community decision is made, in which some rabbis are not consulted. Recently a Federation Council of a large city, which had made it a practice to avoid nominating rabbis for its board, received a rude awakening when a public write-in vote elected three rabbis to that board. Every rabbi, of course, has his own predilection and causes in which he assumes a more than nominal interest, where he is more than a statistic on a membership list.

Certainly, a part of every rabbi's commitment is to the rabbinical organization of both his movement and the community. The Board of Rabbis of his town, whether it consists of three or thirty members, represents the single voice of the Jewish clergy of that city. A wise rabbi cultivates meaningful friendships with his colleagues. When rabbis stand together on matters of vital concern to the spiritual health and welfare of their community, they represent a force with which the community must reckon. Individually and collectively, the rabbis should be the religious and moral backbone of their community. If they succeed in this endeavor, their authority will be far-reaching and their effect will be felt.

## FINDING YOUR OWN LEVEL

Rabbi Jacob Weinstein concluded a recent essay:

> The fact is that there are more than enough shared issues and great purposes to challenge any rabbi to dedicate his heart and his energies. Whether they will lead to a great rabbinic career is not the important question. The question is, Will it help to move mankind a little closer to the good society? A rabbi who demands that his profession bring him greatness in the sense of prominence and prestige is really in the wrong calling. A rabbi who sees no greatness even in the humble tasks of his ministry to a congregation, in his sermons, his pastoral calls, his ceremonial and honorific chores, will not achieve greatness in the larger arena. A rabbi who does not get supreme satisfaction from having helped others on the road to greatness will never achieve it himself. . . . The horizon is full of great issues. They are larger than a man's fist, so that any Elijah can read even while he runs. A rabbi who does not see the bush burning at his very feet, nor feel the fire in his gut, nor hear the call in every vagrant mind, cannot be sincere. His ears are waxed. His eyes are blinded from looking outside for the glory which he should find within.

In these telling words, Rabbi Weinstein enjoins every colleague to find his own level and realize his own capacities and then work to develop these to the utmost. It is wise for the rabbi to take stock of his professional assets and liabilities. It is important for the young rabbi, in particular, to work diligently to strengthen whatever gifts he has and to bring into prominence the unusual capacities which give some contour and structure to his rabbinate.

An important question in conjunction with finding his own level is, Where does the rabbi wish to establish himself? Sometimes, personal considerations determine in what part of the country the rabbi will settle. He may be drawn to the prospect of a large or a small congregation. As might be expected, the greatest number of rabbis is found in large cities, where big congregations abound. Yet there are many who prefer to serve congregations in smaller communities. In these situations, the rabbi might very well find himself the only Jewish clergyman in town. Under no other set of circumstances does the rabbi find himself to be needed as much. He is often the exemplar of the Jewish faith to the non-Jewish community, and its representative. His advice and assistance are sought on all types of communal projects, Jewish and secular. His life may be less hectic than that of his colleagues in the larger centers of population, and usually he knows his people and participates in their lives more intimately.

Many accomplished rabbis, who now serve large metropolitan synagogues, started in the smaller towns off the beaten track. The years of preparation and training that such opportunities afford are immeasurable in terms of their benefit to vocational growth and success. In other instances, rabbis gravitate directly toward large clusters of Jewish population. These areas yield the most extensive opportunities for service and involvement in an active Jewish community with its established schools and communal institutions. The rabbinate in the big city provides much variation. A man may choose to be the spiritual leader of a small, or smaller, congregation in the suburbs; or in time, with proper seniority and seasoning, of a large metropolitan congregation. There are certain rigors that the rabbi in the big town must undergo. He may drive as much as a hundred miles, fulfilling a day's responsibilities, to hospital calls, cemeteries, weddings, and meetings. The necessity of budgeting time becomes very important under such circumstances. Yet no matter how well the rabbi accomplishes this task, he will be forever frustrated, simply because there are only seven days in a week and some sixteen or eighteen waking hours in the day. It is therefore important for the rabbi to learn how to discipline himself and to establish priorities within his work. Much like an old-time movie serial, no matter how much the rabbi does, the ending is always "to be continued."

Rabbi Richard C. Hertz, rabbi of a large congregation, raises the questions:

> What distinguishes a rabbi in a large congregation from one serving in a small community? Is it by the number of weddings at which he officiates? Is it by the number of hospital calls and sick calls and condolence calls he makes? Is it by the number of consultations in the rabbi's study on marital problems, family problems, teenage problems, personal problems, community problems, organizational problems?

It is clearly indicated that volume and accelerated pace characterize the rabbinate of a large congregation in a metropolis. The pastoral rabinate of the big city is no different in substance from that of the small suburban city. Rabbi Hertz, in discussing this point, observes:

> People are people. . . . The rabbi's life is with people. During the course of the day, he may preach and teach, he may pray and play, he may laugh and cry, he may go from a funeral to a wedding reception to a hospital room . . . While some men deal in steel, some in stone, some in dollars, some in goods, a rabbi deals with human hearts. . . . A congrega-

tion is, after all, people, not a building, not an edifice, not a
new temple nor an old temple, but people of all ages, of all
interests and lack of interest.

The rabbinate must be qualitative, whatever the activities and
their number. The temptation to view as so many statistics the
weddings, funerals, bar-mitzvas, and other ritual-centered duties
of the rabbi is ever-present. Because of the pressure of his work,
it is a constant challenge to him to view each event in terms
of its individual importance. For example, the rabbi may be per-
forming his thousandth wedding, but his ceremony for this couple ought not reflect a routinized impersonal procedure. The
rabbi must always make himself aware that for *that* couple it is
their *first* wedding. All the warmth and spontaneity the rabbi
can summon is needed to make the ceremony meaningful. The
same condition holds true for the other rabbinic duties and rites.
His teaching and administrative capacity, as well as his ability
to make the ritual aspects of Jewish life vital, represent the
indices of the rabbi's effectiveness. The rabbi needs to take his
people's problems seriously but himself not too seriously. As
Rabbi Hertz notes, a rabbi can wear any kind of shirt—but-
toned-down, tab, blue, white, or dress shirt—but he can never
wear "a stuffed shirt." That's good advice, important to remember even in the most prestigious moments of a rabbi's career.

Finding one's own level in the rabbinate is the result of conscious resolve, trial and error, and circumstance. For instance,
there were rabbis who intended to accept the call to certain positions only as temporary posts. Twenty years later they were still
in the same pulpit. This was not due to inertia but to the choice
they made to respond to growing challenges that were not
initially anticipated. The fabled Rabbi Henry Cohen (1810-
1875) was known as "the man who stayed in Texas." This
pioneer rabbi chose the difficult task of bringing Judaism to a
frontier of American life. He "stayed" to finish his work. Other
rabbis move from congregation to congregation until they find a
compatible one. Whether in the smaller communities or in the

larger cities, the rabbi should strive to develop his own strong interests. These may be his temple exclusively, serious scholarship, civic life, or some combination of these activities. The rabbi finds fulfilment in his work as long as he remains productive. His own reservoir of talents, enthusiasm and dedication need to be constantly replenished so that his work remains finely honed.

It is for energizing interest in Jewish life and existence that the rabbi was ordained. His road is not an easy one; it is filled with thorns as well as roses, stumbling blocks as well as milestones. Inclement weather of discouragement may threaten the benevolent sunshine of friendship and promise. Yet for a good number of Jewish idealists it is the only road which they choose to walk, for they have that deep and abiding feeling within them, "For this I was created."

CHAPTER V

## The Rabbi and the Future
## of the American Jew

A new climate of opinion is sweeping America with regard to Jews and Judaism. When I grew up as a youngster on the streets of New York, Jews were "out" of the stream of social acceptance in this country. It was an age of quotas and restrictions in housing and universities, in social clubs and in economic opportunities. That era is over to a large extent, and the American Jew today lives in an environment which has been glowingly described by Rabbi Jacob R. Marcus:

> In no instance has he (the Jew) encountered the situation similar to that in this great land where his every hope and yearning is in full consonance with those of his neighbors, where the ideals for which he has in the past sacrificed life and possessions form the very cornerstone of its structure, and where his participation in the common weal is assured as of right rather than by sufferance.

In short, to be Jewish today is to be "in."

Such an environment as we live in presents a fertile field for the planting of Jewish values. Within the last five years we have read the debates on whether or not the Jew was "vanishing." It is concluded in the discussions that the Jew will vanish only if he loses his Jewish consciousness which, while difficult to define, is readily recognizable when it is encountered. This consciousness involves the conviction that one is part of a great people which has had an illustrious yet trying history. Within that history there are marked eras in which Judaism

118

was on the decline, and others in which it was in great efflo-
rescence. There were golden ages and dark ages, ages of persecution as well as of freedom. The deep knowledge of the history of the Jewish people is part of Jewish consciousness. There
is, in addition, the awareness that we live in an ordered world.
Jews have taught the notion of the fatherhood of God and its
derivative principle, the brotherhood of man. Jews have taught
the need for social justice in the world and have been involved
in the critical upheavals which have led to the advance of
human civilization.

It is the rabbi's obligation to perpetuate the Jewish consciousness and to deepen it in successive generations of Jews
by his personal example and his teaching. All the rabbi's skills,
learned through years of hard experience, as well as the vast
fund of knowledge, secular and sacred, which he has garnered,
are to be devoted to this primary task. As we move into a
new era of technocracy, the rabbinate will be faced with the
task of assimilating the insights and methods of this new development in western civilization, and harmonizing it with
the historic truths of Judaism. The rabbis will have to remain
zealous, to see that the computer age does not lead to computarized feelings, computarized allegiances, computarized love
—in short, the snuffing out of the human element in man.

Unquestionably, changes will have to be made in the structure
of Jewish organizational life. Principles of unity, rather than diversity, will be emphasized. Common goals and programs will
be the aim. Manheim Shapiro, director of the Jewish Communal
Affairs department of the American Jewish Committee, has observed that:

> The Jewish group should be held together not merely by
> ethnocentricity but also by a content—a religion, a culture, a
> morality, a distinct style of life, or a combination of some or
> all of these—which enriches the lives of its individual mem-
> bers, the group as a whole, and the surrounding society. This
> content, to be Jewish, must be derived from that entire stream

of development which is called Jewish history, Jewish culture, Jewish creativity, Jewish response to the world and to the universe.

By training and predilection, the rabbi is that singular individual in Jewish society who is able and ready to address himself to the emerging needs of American Jewry and American culture.

While Israel is a political state, it is also the spiritual and cultural center of world Jewry. Because of the decimation of the religious and secular institutions of Russian Jewry, only the American Jew stands on an equal footing with the Jew in Israel, in terms of his capacity to create a meaningful Jewish life. Israeli life and letters already have made a great impression on American Jewry. Hebrew has been reborn as a living tongue. As Israelis are making an attempt to understand diaspora Jewry, so American Jewry must come to grips with developments in Israel. Intellectual currents are never contained by artificial geographic borders. With the interchange of students between our two countries, of professors and of ideologies, Israelis will move into ever closer orbit to the thinking of the American Jew and vice versa. Living bridges of people, traveling freely between these two centers of Jewish civilization, will create a strong bond between us.

Rabbi Max Nussbaum, among many others, has indicated that there is much that Israeli Jewry can learn from American Jewry, particularly in regard to the freedom of its religious life. Both philosophically and structurally, religious Judaism has become a force in America because the bedrock of its development was freedom of conscience. The American rabbi of the Conservative and Reform traditions has few counterparts in Israel. Non-Orthodox Judaism in Israel is in its fledgling state but it will grow because it is within the nature of Judaism itself to promote democratic institutions rather than oligarchies.

The rabbi also has an obligation to world Jewry. A rabbi who loves his people will embrace the Yemenite, the Indian, the North African Jew, as his brother; he is concerned for his fate and the future of his existence. This inevitably propels the American rabbi into activities which will make it possible for Jews in all parts of the world to perpetuate themselves. Generalizing from his experience in America, the rabbi will come to the conclusion that democratic institutions must be assured and supported throughout the world. Jews are the barometers of history. In lands of persecution, where there is restraint on the freedom of thought and belief, Jews and Judaism are among first to suffer. Wherever there is divisiveness and hatred, the Jew is caught in the vise of antagonistic parties. It is in the interest of the American rabbi, both as a matter of principle and hard reality, to promote the idea of a world community to assure basic human rights. Such, after all, was the vision of the Hebrew prophet who dreamt of a world free of war, in which the family of man could dwell together with "none to make them afraid."

As interfaith, interracial, and intercultural activities abound in the "ecumenical age," the universal teachings of Judaism will be found to have particular relevance. The rabbi will, in fact, be devoting himself not only to teaching the mandates of Judaism to his own people, but through them and others, to the widest periphery in our world. Judaism has always been a religion which underscored its mission to teach the Torah to the world. The rabbi, as teacher of that tradition, has both the enormous opportunity and responsibility to expand and continue the system of truths evolved by the Jewish people in its encounter with God and the world. Trained to serve his people, the rabbi can bring these teachings to fruition. Rabbi Abba Hillel Silver taught, "The mission ideal . . . is of the very warp and woof of prophetic Judaism. It is valid today. It is the burden of our destiny . . ." This, in substance, remains the mandate of the modern American rabbi. It is a hard, challenging, historic task. Perhaps you are one who should respond to it.

# Names and Addresses of Seminaries

Candidates for admission to rabbinical seminaries will find it helpful to write to the schools of their choice for further information and catalogs.

## REFORM

Hebrew Union College– Jewish Institute of Religion (HUC-JIR)
Clifton Ave.
Cincinnati, Ohio 45220

Hebrew Union College– Jewish Institute of Religion
40 W. 68th Street
New York, N.Y. 10023

Hebrew Union College– Jewish Institute of Religion
8745 Appian Way
Los Angeles, Calif. 90046

Hebrew Union College Biblical and Archaeological School
13 King David Street
Jerusalem, Israel

## CONSERVATIVE

Jewish Theological Seminary (JTS)
3080 Broadway
New York, N.Y. 10027

## ORTHODOX

Yeshiva University
Rabbi Isaac Elchanan Theological Seminary (RIETS)
186th Street and Amsterdam Ave.
New York, N.Y. 10033

Jewish University of America
(formerly Hebrew Theological College)
7135 N. Carpenter Road
Skokie, Ill. 60076

Mesivta Yeshiva
Rabbi Chaim Berlin Rabbinical Academy
350 Stone Ave.
Brooklyn, N.Y. 11212

Ner Israel Rabbinical College
4411 Garrison Blvd.
Baltimore, Md. 21215

Rabbinical College of Telshe
28440 Euclid Ave.
Wickliffe, Ohio 44092

United Lubavitcher Yeshivoth
Bedford Ave. and Dean Street
Brooklyn, N.Y. 11216

West Coast Talmudical Seminary
Mesivta Beth Midrash Elyon Inc.
11027 Burbank Blvd.
North Hollywood, Calif. 91601

Yavneh Hebrew Theological Seminary
510 Dahill Road
Brooklyn, N.Y. 11218

Yeshiva Torah Vodaath and Mesivta Rabbinical Seminary
141 S. Third Street
Brooklyn, N.Y. 11211

## ALLIED ORGANIZATIONS

B'nai B'rith Hillel Foundations Inc.
1640 Rhode Island Ave.
Washington, D.C. 20036

Central Conference of American Rabbis (CCAR)
790 Madison Ave.
New York, N.Y. 10021

Jewish Reconstructionist Foundation
15 W. 86th Street
New York, N.Y. 10024

Rabbinical Alliance of America (Orthodox)
154 Nassau Street
New York, N.Y. 10038

Rabbinical Assembly (Conservative) (RA)
3080 Broadway
New York, N.Y. 10027

Rabbinical Council of America (Orthodox) (RCA)
84 Fifth Ave.
New York, N.Y. 10011

Synagogue Council of America (Inter-denominational)
235 Fifth Ave.
New York, N.Y. 10016

Union of American Hebrew
Congregations (Reform)
(UAHC)
838 Fifth Ave.
New York, N.Y. 10021

Union of Orthodox Jewish
Congregations of Amer-
ica (UOJC)
84 Fifth Ave.
New York, N.Y. 10011

Union of Orthodox Rabbis
of the United States and
Canada
235 E. Broadway
New York, N.Y. 10002

United Synagogue of Amer-
ica (Conservative)
(USA)
3080 Broadway
New York, N.Y. 10027

American Jewish Correc-
tional Chaplains Associa-
tion
10 E. 73rd Street
New York, N.Y. 10021

Commission on Jewish
Chaplaincy (National
Jewish Welfare Board)
145 E. 32nd Street
New York, N.Y. 10016

APPENDIX B

# List of Abbreviations

| | |
|---|---|
| CCAR | Central Conference of American Rabbis |
| CSD | Community Service Division (Yeshiva University) |
| HUC-JIR | Hebrew Union College–Jewish Institute of Religion |
| JTS | Jewish Theological Seminary |
| JWB | Jewish Welfare Board |
| RIETS | Rabbi Isaac Elchanan Theological Seminary |
| RA | Rabbinical Assembly |
| RCA | Rabbinical Council of America |
| UAHC | Union of American Hebrew Congregations |
| UOJC | Union of Orthodox Jewish Congregations |
| USA | United Synagogue of America |